FENG SHUI

HOME DESIGN

AND COLORS

Living Room, Kitchen, Dining Room, Bedroom, Bathroom, Children's Room, Office, And Garden

By AMY LANDRY

Copyright © 2021 AMY LANDRY All rights reserved.

No part of this guide may be reproduced in any form without permission in writing from the publisher except in the case of brief quotations embodied in critical chapters or reviews.

Legal & Disclaimer

The information contained in this book and its contents is not designed to replace or take the place of any form of medical or professional advice; and is not meant to replace the need for independent medical, financial, legal or other professional advice or services, as may be required. The content and information in this book have been provided for educational and entertainment purposes only.

The content and information contained in this book has been compiled from sources deemed reliable, and it is accurate to the best of the Author's knowledge, information and belief. However, the Author cannot guarantee its accuracy and validity and cannot be held liable for any errors and/or omissions. Further, changes are periodically made to this book as and when needed. Where appropriate and/or necessary, you must consult a professional (including but not limited to your doctor, attorney, financial advisor or such other professional advisor) before using any of the suggested remedies, techniques, or information in this book.

Upon using the contents and information contained in this book, you agree to hold harmless the Author from and against any damages, costs, and expenses, including any legal fees potentially resulting from the application of any of the information provided by this book. This disclaimer applies to any loss, damages or injury caused by the use and application, whether directly or indirectly, of any advice or information presented, whether for breach of contract, tort, negligence, personal injury, criminal intent, or under any other cause of action.

You agree to accept all risks of using the information presented inside this book.

You agree that by continuing to read this book, where appropriate and/or necessary, you shall consult a professional (including but not limited to your doctor, attorney, or financial advisor or such other advisor as needed) before using any of the suggested remedies, techniques, or information in this book.

SOMMARIO

INTRODUCTION 5
    FENG SHUI IN INTERIOR DESIGN: FEATURES AND MATERIALS TO USE 8

HISTORICAL ROOTS AND PHILOSOPHICAL FOUNDATIONS OF FENG SHUI.... 12

FURNITURE: FENG SHUI DESIGN 17

IS YOUR BEDROOM POSITIONED CORRECTLY ACCORDING TO FENG SHUI?. 22
    FENG SHUI: THE ORIENTATION OF THE BED TO SLEEP WELL 26
    THE FAVORABLE AND UNFAVORABLE PERSONAL DIRECTIONS AND THE EIGHT PALACES METHOD 31

COLORS ACCORDING TO THE PHILOSOPHY OF FENG- SHUI LIVING............... 38
    THE RIGHT COLOR FOR EVERY ROOM 39
    SIMPLE DIRECTIONS TO CHOOSE THE RIGHT COLOR! 40
        green 41
        red 42
        Yellow and brown 42
        White 43
        The blue tones 43
        The effects of color 43
        Colors in spatial perception 44

HOW TO FURNISH A LIVING ROOM IN FENG SHUI STYLE: PRACTICAL TIPS TO FOLLOW 46

FENG SHUI TALISMANS AND AMULETS 49
    FOR HEALTH AND LONGEVITY 50
    FOR WEALTH AND PROSPERITY 51
    FOR THE WELL-BEING OF THE FAMILY 53
    FOR CAREER AND GOOD LUCK 54
    WHERE TO PUT THEM? 55

BAGUA MAP AND FENG SHUI 56

- Art, philosophy or science? 56
- How to use the Bagua map 59
- Feng Shui: the Bagua map to distinguish environments 60

FENG SHUI AND BIOARCHITECTURE 63

FENG SHUI: 10 TIPS FOR DECORATING YOUR HOME WITH AWARENESS 67

- Constructive Principles of Feng Shui 70

THE FENG SHUI GARDEN. THE ANCIENT CHINESE ART OF MAKING ENERGIES FLOW INTO SPACE 73

> Bring balance and harmony to the home with the art of Feng Shui, placing the emphasis on the environment around us and on well-being. 77

TIDY UP YOUR HOME TO ATTRACT WEALTH, LOVE, HEALTH 80

- LET'S CLEAN, TIDY, AND USE THE RIGHT REMEDIES 82

BAGUA METHOD TO ATTRACT LUCK IN THE DIFFERENT SECTORS OF THE HOUSE 84

FENG SHUI: THE PRINCIPLES AND RULES OF THE ANCIENT CHINESE DISCIPLINE 87

10 THINGS NOT TO HAVE AT HOME ACCORDING TO FENG SHUI 90

WHAT ARE THE GOOD (AND BAD) PLANTS FOR FENG SHUI? 93

- Feng Shui And Plants in The House: The Ideal Locations 95

FURNISH SMALL HOUSES WITH FENG SHUI 97

THE FIVE ELEMENTS IN FENG SHUI 101

- The Cycles of the Five Elements: 101

CONCLUSION 111

FENG SHUI: HOME DESIGN AND COLORS

INTRODUCTION

WHAT IS FENG SHUI AND WHAT ARE ITS RULES?

IT IS IDEAL FOR A HARMONIOUS HOME THAT CONVEYS SERENITY

Why not try the Feng Shui method to have a home furnished in a harmonious way which transmits serenity to those who live there? Here are the fundamental principles of this oriental practice that has important repercussions on our daily life.

Feng shui seeks harmony in the home, in furniture arrangement, lighting, beds, plants and everything that makes up an apartment.

This is the goal of an oriental discipline that has recently begun to be widespread also in the West. Until about ten years ago, architects and interior designers worked on the aesthetic factor to furnish a home. However, no particular attention was paid to the problem of energy forces that can be blocked by walls or furniture in a specific place.

This is the main concern of those who buy a house in the East, especially in China, where Feng Shui was founded thousands of years ago, where houses are examined above all, according to energy standards. And even those who want to build a home require that the facade and the main entrance face south, or that there are streams nearby: water brings wealth. Or even that the inside of the house does not have excessively sharp angles that block the flow of energy.

What is feng shui?

According to Feng Shui, which literally means "wind and water", harmony depends on the balance between the two principles of the whole, Yin and Yang.

They are two opposing forces that dominate the universe and are typical of Chinese and Eastern culture in general.

FENG SHUI: HOME DESIGN AND COLORS

Yin recalls the female sex, the earth and the moon, passivity and dark colors.

Yang recalls the male sex, the sun, light colors, heat.

If Yang prevails, the environment is stimulating but, in the workplace, it can be stressful.

If Yin prevails, the work environment can be downright depressing.

Furnishing with Feng Shui

This is about considering the natural signals of the environment. In every environment there are energies, called Chi, which interact positively with a person; *stimulate, soothe, instill optimism, courage, self- confidence*.

However, if something stands between these sources, the energies are blocked.

A practical example based on Feng Shui is that of a house door that opens with difficulty, it blocks energy and - amazingly - can negatively affect your career!

Furnishing tips

In practice, here are some furnishing tips:

- If the walls are white, it is necessary to contrast this with objects of dark colors and make natural light prevail over artificial light, introducing natural elements such as plants, stones, and pieces of wood.
- It is also better to use pink Himalayan salt lamps, scented candles made from virgin beeswax and aromatic sticks to propitiate positive energy and relaxation.

Feng Shui And Bagua

In China and Japan, Feng Shui experts use a map called Bagua which is compared with the floor plan of the house or office. If the latter does not coincide with the Bagua it is necessary to intervene.

FENG SHUI: HOME DESIGN AND COLORS

Feng Shui And the Mirror

To propitiate energy, it is useful to place mirrors on the walls or on the desk; they reject negative energies but are a source of stimulation so they must be eliminated in the bedroom.

Feng shui and the bedroom

To bring the bedroom back into balance and ensure peaceful sleep, we can try to eliminate objects that are not used for sleep, since we spend almost only the night there. So put away the mess, the objects crammed under the bed and those things around the room that are used for other purposes, such as the computer for work and the mobile phone.

It is also good to place the bed on the wall furthest from the door but 'in the command position', i.e., with the headboard facing the entrance, but attached to a solid wall and preferably with no openings.

Then remove the mirrors, which stimulate energy and prevent relaxation.

Feng Shui In the Office

Although it is a deep and complex philosophy, some rules are simple. As we will see, they can also be put into practice in an office environment.

Here too, in fact, the rule of eliminating the disorder applies, especially at the entrance, which should be simple and free of obstacles, because here the energy flows. A simple light outside and a visible nameplate help to rebalance the energy.

The color of the walls must follow the principles of feng shui but with an eye to the type of profession carried out in the office.

The desks must not face the door or the windows, in order not to attract negative energies: a solid wall is better! And if that's not possible, a mirror can be used to reflect the entrance.

FENG SHUI: HOME DESIGN AND COLORS

Finally, always locate the command position, for example the northernmost chair, the farthest desk from the entrance, which give more power.

Putting these tips into practice does not cost much and perhaps our mood will benefit from it, both at home and in the office!

FENG SHUI IN INTERIOR DESIGN: FEATURES AND MATERIALS TO USE

There are numerous styles when it comes to interior design, some represent evergreens, others follow trends dictated by designers or influential personalities in the sector. In this article we will deepen the Feng Shui style in interior design, an oriental practice with a strong mystical character that is widely taking hold in the West.

The meaning of Feng Shui is very profound: literally Feng Shui means "wind and water", two extremely opposed natural elements, but on whose balance the harmony between Yin and Yang depends, in oriental culture forces that dominate the universe. In other words, Feng Shui applied to interior design seeks harmony in domestic environments through various factors: the arrangement of the furniture, the lighting, the presence of plants and everything that is part of the composition of a domestic or working environment.

That of Feng Shui, although it is a millenary discipline and has always been inherent in Eastern culture, is an absolute novelty for the Western world. If in the East the choice of a home depends almost exclusively on factors linked to positive energy, in the West, architects and interior designers have never been as willing as they are today, in addition to working on the aesthetic factor in the choice of furniture or the arrangement of a house, to also consider the aspects that this "new" oriental discipline suggests, as if to favor a better circulation of "positive forces" within the environment.

To give some examples, in China (where Feng Shui was founded) some of the criteria that determine the appearance of a house are:

FENG SHUI: HOME DESIGN AND COLORS

- the exposure of the main facade facing south
- the proximity of waterways, a sign of wealth
- the inside of the house must not have excessively sharp angles, which would block the flow of energy

CREATING FENG SHUI FURNITURE: MAIN FEATURES

According to the discipline of Feng Shui, in every home or work environment there are energies that interact and positively stimulate the people who live/work in the space: they can foster optimism, cheer up, instill courage and confidence, but nothing must overlap between these sources to prevent its correct dissemination. In China and Japan experts of the Feng Shui discipline use the Bagua, a particular map that serves to verify that the arrangement of the house or workplace favors the circulation of these positive energies.

Feng Shui furniture has the following characteristics:

- Contrast of light and dark colors. For example, if the walls are white, it is good to contrast with dark colored furniture
- Natural lighting. It is recommended to illuminate the rooms with natural light and that these prevail over artificial light sources.
- Natural elements. Plants, wooden elements, stones must be inserted into the environment to magnetize the energy flows.
- Essences and perfumes. According to the oriental discipline, the use of natural essences and particular fragrances is suggested as propitiatory elements of positive energy.
- The mirror. Feng Shui considers the mirror as a useful element to reject negative energies. It should be placed in passageways or environments such as the living room, but not in the bedroom, as it would not favor rest.

The workplace is also subject to discipline by Feng Shui. An environment such as the office is now lived in for several hours of the day and therefore requires a certain comfort and a certain livability, useful to create a pleasant place that favors collaboration between colleagues.

FENG SHUI: HOME DESIGN AND COLORS

Feng Shui for the office must respect the following characteristics:

- Order. Especially at the entrance to the office there must be strict order, which will not cause obstacles to the flow of positive energy.
- Light colors vs Dark colors. As in Feng Shui furniture for the home, even in the office there must be the right balance between light colors and dark colors. Sometimes this also depends on the profession performed.
- The arrangement of the desks. Feng Shui advises against arranging desks with their backs to doors and windows as this would attract negative energy.

THE MATERIALS OF FENG SHUI: FROM WOOD TO METALS

In Feng Shui the materials play a fundamental role in the diffusion of energies in the environment (calledChi). Among the main materials we find: wood, fabric, plastic, stones and bricks, metals, glass.

Wood in Feng Shui

Being of vegetable origin, wood is very important in Feng Shui furnishings; it is considered as a living material with polyvalent characteristics and can be used in any room of the house.

Fabric in Feng Shui

Fabrics (in particular natural fibers such as linen, silk, cotton and wool) according to the discipline of Feng Shui must be used not excessively and in particular in places of relaxation, since their composition (woven and padded) would slow down the flow of energies.

Plastic in Feng Shui

FENG SHUI: HOME DESIGN AND COLORS

Plastic is a synthetic material and that is why, according to the oriental discipline, it should be used moderately so as not to cause a blocking effect of the energies within the environment.

Bricks and stones in Feng Shui

Although these are natural materials, their conformation means that a moderate and orderly use is suggested. Inside it is good to use stones with a more solid composition and a shiny appearance, outside porous and opaque stones (such as travertine, slate, etc. ..). These materials are not recommended in areas such as the bedroom.

Metal and glass in Feng Shui

Metals are also important in Feng Shui and have different characteristics based on their composition: if shiny and reflective, like glass, they are suitable for places to relax; otherwise, they would favor a greater flow of energy and should be used in more dynamic places.

The colors of Feng Shui

To conclude, a brief insight into the colors that the Feng Shui discipline prefers: the choice must not be random but designed for each environment. In an area like the living room, warm colors like red and orange can help conversation with guests or family members. Shades such as blue and green favor relaxation and consequently sleep, so they are to be used in bedrooms; yellow, on the other hand, stimulates the appetite and provides the necessary energy from the beginning of the day.

FENG SHUI: HOME DESIGN AND COLORS

HISTORICAL ROOTS AND PHILOSOPHICAL FOUNDATIONS OF FENG SHUI

To understand what Feng Shui is and understand why it is still a useful tool today, we must go back in time, to its origins, to the golden age of Chinese thought. The predynastic period of the Eastern Zhou (771 BC - 221 BC), "five centuries in which there was only a semblance of central authority, was an era of dynamic development, during which great energies and a grandiose creative spirit, an age that is unmatched in any other subsequent period of Chinese history. Perhaps the multiplicity of states and their rivalries acted as a stimulus".

During this period China recovers the technological disadvantage compared to the cultures of Middle East Asia and the Mediterranean basin: the introduction of iron in the work of the fields and the control of water for irrigation initiate a real agricultural revolution that reflects demographic growth, the rapid development of trade and an enormous increase in wealth. We must imagine this era as a kind of renaissance with a great flourishing of ideas, sages, heroes and brigands, during which the various small states into which China was still divided (the unification of China takes place in 221 BC by Qin Shi Huangdi), vied for the services of professional teachers, thinkers, philosophers and bureaucrats; people traveled continuously from one state to another and ideas traveled with men.

Each aristocratic family also kept with them experts in occultism, called fang shi (the literal translation is "gentlemen with recipes" meaning people who, with their knowledge, were able to find solutions to problems), who practiced the Six Occult Arts: astrology, the almanacs, the five elements, the I Ching, various other divination methods and the system of form which later took the name of Feng Shui; they passed on the art from father to son and were consulted on every important occasion. With the social changes at the end of the Zhou era and the disintegration of the aristocracy, many of the fang shi were forced to abandon their patrons and wander the country in search of employment, sometimes even among the people.

FENG SHUI: HOME DESIGN AND COLORS

Starting from this period the philosophical interest of the Chinese focuses on man, in stark contrast to the importance attributed to the divine and to the otherworldly world by the philosophies of India and many Mediterranean civilizations. Despite having Shang Di and Tian as supreme deities and believing in the existence of a large number of spirits and supernatural beings, the Chinese of the Zhou era focused their interest mainly on man and his relationships with the surrounding social environment, but rather than attaching importance to the individual, they took man into consideration as a member of society.

Two main currents emerge around the fourth century BC, Confucianism, which focuses on ethically irreproachable conduct, on the balance between inner virtues and outer behavior, on order and respect for rituals and relationships, and Taoism, mainly a philosophy of protest, the rebellion of the common man against the growing despotism of the rulers, and the rebellion of the uncommon man, gifted with intelligence and sensitivity, against the growing rigidity of moralists. The Taoists firmly defended the independence of the individual whose only concern was to adapt to the great model of nature and to achieve the union of man with an impersonal natural order.

Feng Shui fits into this context, which seeks harmony between man and the surrounding environment. When it abandons the belief in supernatural forces and tries to interpret the universe, occultism then turns into science, in terms of natural forces through the study of landscape, seasons, climate and celestial cycles to understand the environment. Astrology, Yi Jing, almanacs and the five elements come together in Feng Shui. The theory of the Five Elements, in Chinese, Wu Xing, appears for the first time in a text which, according to tradition, dates back to the 12th century BC and is attributed to the mythical king Yu, founder of the kingdom of Xia in the 22nd century BC; the invention of the compass is also attributed to a mythological ruler, Huang Di, known as the Yellow Emperor, legendary Chinese emperor, defined a cultural hero and considered ancestor of all the Han. According to tradition, in 2634 BC he used a chariot with a special wheeled device that caused a statue to always point in the same direction despite the turns made by the vehicle and thanks to which he won an important battle fought in the fog.

Another Feng Shui element that dates back to a protohistoric era is the magic square Lo Shu, which would emerge before the eyes of Emperor Yu of the Xia dynasty, drawn on the carapace of a turtle that at that moment emerged from the waters of the Yellow River.

It is probable that Taoism has absorbed the previous traditions and reworked them in an organic way in the classical works we know today, among the most important, the Dao De Jing of the 6th century BC and the Chuang Zi of the 4th century BC. The concept of virtue understood as not performing any action contrary to nature following the principle of wei wu wei, that is "doing what not doing".

The Taoists also developed the theory of the microcosm reflected in the macrocosm, a theory that modern mathematics has codified today. The property of reproducing oneself from small to large is called self - similarity - a part of the object is similar to the whole. In geometry, objects that are self-similar are defined as fractals and can be constructed following precise mathematical rules and expressed with the following formula:

Let us consider a set of N transformations (not necessarily affine) of the Cartesian plane: $\{T_1, T_2, T_3, ..., T_N\}$ and apply them to the same subset A of the plane. As a result, we will obtain a family of N subsets of the Cartesian plane $\{T_1(A), T_2(A), T_3(A), ..., T_N(A)\}$.

Let A_1 be the set obtained as a union of these subsets. Let us again apply the N transformations to the set A_1 thus obtained and consider the union of the N image sets. We call this together A_2. We act in the same way on A_2 and we get A_3.

We can therefore say that the fractal formula, which scientifically codifies a philosophical speculation of 400 BC, makes Feng Shui a rigorous discipline and no longer associated with magic.

Over the centuries the fang shi have continued to operate and serve aristocrats, officials and emperors, and in Asia in fact they have never stopped, but over time this art has evolved to the point that, in the Song era (960-1279 AD), two currents were born: the "School of the compass" and the "School of form". The first perfected the use of the "geomantic compass", which consisted of a disk with a magnetic needle in the center; the outer concentric circles contained the Eight trigrams, the Five Phases and the indicators of the Chinese duodecimal calendar, the Terrestrial Branches and the Celestial Steles, as well as other astronomical and cosmological indices. The followers of the form were more tied to the concrete qualities of the landscape, which the expert traversed and carefully scrutinized to find the hidden currents in the earth, defined as "Veins of Dragons", which should not be damaged by buildings. Both schools were based on the same principle: to construct buildings in such a way that they were integrated into the environment instead of dominating it.

But what happens today? Contemporary societies are based on living and working in crowded urban environments, where the pace of life is extremely fast and our bond with the planet is now almost buried in concrete. However, the "dragon veins" are still pulsating and our homes feel their strength today as they did in ancient China once upon a time.

We must imagine that the house is a living entity, it must breathe, it must receive a sufficient quantity of energy that is also of good quality; it is influenced by the external configurations and the orientation of the doors that guide the Chi into and out of the dwelling. Traditional Feng Shui aims to achieve the union of the Yin Energy (Earth Energy) with the Yang Energy (Celestial Energy) inside the house, based on a meticulous and detailed calculation connected to the planetary movements that serves to recognize the energy conformations present and to harmonize them if necessary.

The most powerful of all Feng Shui styles is called " Yuen Hom " or "Mystery of the Void". This style of Feng Shui was consistently applied in the Chinese Imperial Courts during many dynasties, and is based on a vast and complex interpretation of the 64 Hexagrams of the I Ching, or Book of Changes, which describes all manifestations of the vital energies. Inside the house, through the Yuen Hom style, specific energy centers can be identified, connected to particular types of energy and the life of the occupants. When these energy centers are blocked, the corresponding aspects of the life of the person occupying that house may also be blocked at the same time. Traditional Feng Shui also includes a detailed assessment of the external environment, which specifically affects the individual occupants of a home, as well as having energetic effects on particular limbs and organs of the body.

Through a careful analysis based on Yuen Hom calculations, the consultant is able to access and exploit energy channels, in the same way that acupuncture works, which identifies the Chi channels present in the body and manipulates them by freeing them from blocks. Since every house is the mirror of those who live there, like everything that belongs to us or that is made by us, it tells a little about us, our vision of the world and our experiences and here is the theory of microcosm reflected in the macrocosm; the place where we have chosen to live encodes our sensitivity in a certain sense and says a lot about our personality and character, regardless of whether we are aware of it or not. The consultant reveals these subtle connections and is able to tell us why, at this moment of our life, we choose to live in a particular house, with a specific orientation with certain characteristics, the influences that this house has on us, towards what kind of life our instincts have guided us and the teachings we are ready to receive. With a sort of maieutic work, the consultant thus takes us to a deep level of understanding of our current situation because we are ready to listen, understand, change and take a further step on the path of awareness.

FENG SHUI: HOME DESIGN AND COLORS

FURNITURE: FENG SHUI DESIGN

WHY FENG SHUI

Feng Shui helps us to furnish and create environments that are in harmony with us, bringing happiness and well-being. It is a philosophy that teaches us to respect nature by living in a balanced relationship with it. The positive energy of a healthy and harmonious environment will support our mental, physical and spiritual well-being.

The aim is to make some changes in your home, transforming it into a space of well-being and a source of energy, going to affect certain aspects of your life in a targeted way.

Feng Shui tries to balance the constant flow and movement of Qi, Yin and Yang energy and the five elements: earth, wood, metal, fire and water. If these energies are in balance in our environment, we will be in harmony and balance too.

The five elements of Feng Shui

FENG SHUI: HOME DESIGN AND COLORS

Feng Shui is a very well-known discipline. It is also applied in the West and integrates perfectly with our culture. In fact, to practice Feng Shui it is not necessary to use special Chinese objects, but it is enough to use the ideas of this discipline to have a positive effect on our well-being.

FENG SHUI TOOLS

By furnishing your home according to your personal tastes and with the most suitable furniture and colors, you will create an environment that reflects your being and this will allow you to accumulate well-being and energy.

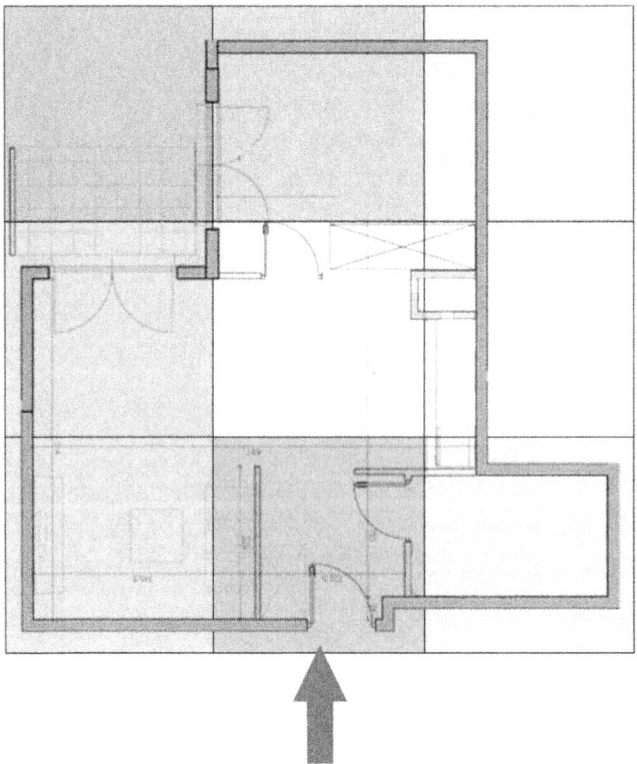

The tools that help us achieve balance come precisely from Feng Shui.

FENG SHUI: HOME DESIGN AND COLORS

For every room in the house there are basic rules to follow but it is possible to use different remedies and techniques to harmonize the environment and promote the flow of energy such as:

- Correct placement of furniture to promote the flow of Chi;
- Adequate lighting of the environment;
- Right combination of colors;
- Decorations and accessories;
- Order and cleanliness;
- Elimination of clutter and disturbing elements;
- Use of symbols bringing good luck;
- Insertion of personal items;
- Furniture and objects that make you feel good.

OBJECTIVES OF FENG SHUI

Thanks to Feng Shui you can:

- achieve psycho-physical well-being thanks to a healthy and welcoming environment;
- creation of serene spaces and organization of children's rooms;
- improve sleep quality with suitable furniture and its correct arrangement;
- work and study with greater concentration;
- reduce stress by reorganizing spaces and eliminating the superfluous;
- optimize the flow of energy by reorganizing the spaces in your home (and consequently in your life).

FENG SHUI: HOME DESIGN AND COLORS

With a view to creating harmonious spaces that give us well-being, the materials that make up the furniture are an aspect to be strongly considered when buying. A conscious choice in favoring furnishings, furniture and fabrics that use natural materials, nowadays has become necessary to obtain a healthy environment. A healthy environment, well-ventilated and free from harmful substances, will provide well-being and health to all members of the family.

AN ANCIENT SCIENCE

Feng Shui is an ancient and complex discipline. Inside, many traditions are intertwined, ranging from rituals to philosophy to medicine. Ancient Asian peoples studied how the energies of nature affected the environment and humans. The origins of this discipline are found in China, considered the cradle of Feng Shui. Its application was part of daily life in both small and large things. The most famous works representing Chinese civilization, such as the Great Wall and the Secret Cities of Beijing, were created following the dictates of Feng Shui. Over the years this discipline has also seen dark periods in which any practice and dissemination was prohibited. Despite this the tradition has survived, bringing to light a priceless heritage of experiences and practices.

FENG SHUI: HOME DESIGN AND COLORS

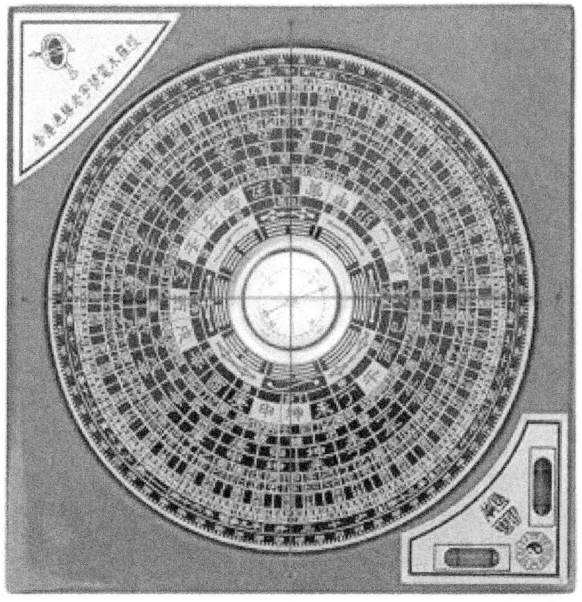

Many of the teachings of Feng Shui were also known in other regions of the world. Every ancient people intuitively knew the regularity of the energy flows of nature and behaved accordingly. However, much information related to the effects of location and orientation, furniture, use of art and colors, was available to a limited number of people, such as guilds and religious brotherhoods. Outside of China, it was not possible to take advantage of this information at the level of the masses, as there was a lack of written texts in the public domain.

Currently Feng Shui is increasingly expanding, and there are also many architects who approach this discipline and its ancient teachings. Feng Shui blends harmoniously with modern Interior Color Design.

FENG SHUI: HOME DESIGN AND COLORS

IS YOUR BEDROOM POSITIONED CORRECTLY ACCORDING TO FENG SHUI?

The bedroom is the most important environment in the home: each of us spends about a third of their lives in bed. In the bedroom - and in the bed - we rest, recover our energies, spend periods of convalescence, experience intimate situations. It is therefore understandable that in Feng Shui the bedroom has a particular relevance.

But it's not just for these reasons ...

All those listed above are already sufficiently important reasons, which prompt us to carefully evaluate the position of the bed and the orientation of the headboard. But there are other deeper motivations as well. Feng Shui teaches us that the place where we sleep, the "bedroom", is the point of origin of the history of the evolution of our homes. It all started, in fact, when one of our ancestors, a long time ago, looked for a cave or a hole in the rocks to shelter, perhaps from a predator, or perhaps simply from the cold.

I know, the bedroom is important, the bed should be positioned with the head to the north etcetera ...

We will deal with these specific aspects, which concern the bed, in other articles (among other things, it is absolutely not true that the bed must be positioned with the head to the north according to Feng Shui!). But now we are talking about the location of the bedroom within the apartment or house. To do this, we take the floor plan of the house and consider the position and direction of the bedroom relative to the front door.

How? What does the position of the bedroom have to do with it?

It has something to do with it, and it is often more important than the position and orientation of the bed within the same room! How is it possible? Very simple: the structure and the location of the living functions (bedrooms, kitchen, entrance, bathrooms, study, ...), as well as the connections between them, are of greater importance than the location of the furnishings within each room. It is like inside the human body: the systems (= set of organs assigned to a specific function, e.g., the immune, digestive system, etc.) have a higher priority level than the single organ. Two organs may be functioning well, but if there is no connection or if they fail to coordinate, the overall effect is not beneficial to the body.

Therefore, in Feng Shui, the position of the bedroom must always be evaluated before the positioning of the bed itself, and the orientation of the head of the bed. Let's now see how Feng Shui considers the bedroom.

What is the bedroom for?

Basically, the room represents an additional protection area, an alcove, compared to a larger protective area that is given by the house itself. Since hearing is the only sense that remains active in sleep, many animals and almost all mammals, when they have to rest for a long time or have to regain their strength after a fight or after an illness, look for sheltered, hidden, not easily accessible places, whose path is full of curves and obstacles. In this way, the animal unknowingly knows that - when it sleeps - it has more time to hear the noises caused by the approach of a potential predator, and to wake up.

If the animal is badly positioned in the recovery phase, its regeneration activity will suffer interference and will be less effective, because part of the energy must be used to keep the environment under control. If nothing else, in unprotected positions it will be necessary to have a lighter sleep in order to have a quicker reaction in case of danger. This "lighter" sleep provides for the alteration of the hormonal balance in favor of the exciting hormones. You can understand very well that this is not ideal when it is necessary to rest and restore strength, quite the opposite of what we would like to have!

For this reason, in Feng Shui the position of the bedroom in the floor plan of the house - and its distance and location from the front door - are almost always more important than the position of the bed itself. So let's look at the most important possibilities.

FENG SHUI: HOME DESIGN AND COLORS

The bed is visible from the front door

This means there is a door-to-bedroom door alignment. This is the least favorable configuration. People who sleep in this bed may feel threatened or have disturbed sleep. The feeling of danger coming from the front door can be just too strong. Sometimes, even knowing that the front door is locked, and the front door to the room is closed, one still feels uncomfortable. Worse still, dominant individuals tend to keep the bedroom door open so they can control the front door. While this can be helpful, it increases the weakness of the position. Feng Shui teaches that this configuration should always be carefully avoided, apart from some special cases in which it is not possible to do otherwise (for example, in a studio apartment); and even in these cases, it is necessary to take appropriate measures.

From the entrance door to the bed, it is necessary to make a right angle

Enter the house and proceed for a few meters, turning right or left you will be able to see the bedroom door. To reach the bed, therefore, it will be sufficient to make a right angle. Even this situation, although much better than the previous one, is not ideal. Visitors may be annoyed and embarrassed, because the bedroom view is associated with intimacy. To solve this problem, simply keep the chamber door closed. However, this does not solve the alignment problem; a right angle is still too little to have a safe position, ideal for sleeping. If it is possible to turn the bed, so that it is not directly accessible from the door without making a further right angle, we arrive in a position that we can consider essentially neutral.

Two right angles

When it is necessary to make two right angles on the way from the front door of the house to the bed, we are in a neutral situation. This is the minimum acceptable from a Feng Shui point of view. Two right angles lengthen the time available enough to perceive the potential danger. Closed bedroom doors can increase the feeling of protection and comfort. Sometimes, if possible, by moving the bed it is possible to move to a much better position, one with three right angles.

Three right angles

If on the way from the front door of the apartment to the bed it is necessary to make three right angles, the position is very good. Three right angles force a possible enemy / predator to slow down three times, and provide a time and distance deemed sufficient for Feng Shui, allowing deep relaxation to those who use the bedroom. Relaxation that will have a positive effect on the well-being of the person, on psychological stability, on the ability to react and on mental acuity, also decreasing irritability.

If there are more than three right angles, the bedroom position is even stronger and more protected.

What have we learned?

- in authentic Feng Shui, the positioning of the bedroom is more important than that of the bed, being of higher priority;
- it is not necessary to always have the head positioned north when sleeping - it is a myth;
- if from the entrance door access to the bed is immediate (alignment of the entrance door - bedroom door - bed), the position is not favorable and it is necessary to intervene using Feng Shui;
- if from the front door it is necessary to make a right angle to reach the bed, the position is still weak but better than the previous one; it is necessary to try to improve the situation, always using Feng Shui;
- if from the front door it is necessary to make two right angles to reach the bed, the position is good enough;
- if from the front door it is necessary to travel through three or more right angles to reach the bed, the position is very good.

FENG SHUI: HOME DESIGN AND COLORS

Of course, these guidelines apply to the bed, not to all important furnishings! One of the most common mistakes found in Feng Shui books is to have confused the positioning methods for yang positions (i.e., those used in a waking state: desk, cash desk, reception desk, etc.) with those for yin positions (bed, relaxation area). But is not so! As it will seem logical to everyone, since these are stations that are used in a very different way, they will be governed by different principles and priorities.

We must not forget that in Feng Shui these considerations must always be integrated with others such as: the position of the bed inside the room, the orientation of the bed, the direction of the head, the colors of the bedroom, the presence of large mirrors in the room, if it is a room for adults or a room for children, etc.

FENG SHUI: THE ORIENTATION OF THE BED TO SLEEP WELL

When we talk about the orientation of the bed, we refer to the geographical orientation (the measurement is taken with a compass, or with the Lo Pan); we do not refer to the Bagua positioned according to the position of the entrance door, a method belonging to the school called 'Buddhist Tantric Sect of Black Caps' and invented around 1985 in California, as it is simply not relevant to authentic Feng Shui.

Also, here we will limit ourselves to 8 directions (north, north east, east, ...), but advanced applications require the use of 24 specific directions, or even more.

The priorities in the bedroom according to Feng Shui

If you have read the two previous articles, you already know that in professional Feng Shui it is incorrect to work with techniques and methods: you must proceed according to principles and priorities. In our case, priority n.1 is to evaluate the position of the room with respect to the entrance door, for obvious safety reasons; priority n.2 is to evaluate the position of the bed with respect to the room; priority # 3 is to evaluate the orientation of the bed (direction of the head of the bed). In this article we will deal with point 3. Later we will also publish an article dedicated specifically to Feng Shui for the children's room.

As you can see, the orientation of the head of the bed has priority 3: this means that if priorities 1 and 2 have been respected, and if we still have a choice between multiple positions, then it is important to choose the best orientation. If, however, by applying Feng Shui priorities 1 and 2 we have found a single possible position for the bed (this almost always happens if the bedroom is not very large), the orientation is already defined and this part can be omitted, with some exceptions which we will discuss later.

Basically, when it comes to sleeping comfort and peace of mind, direction is not very important.

What is meant by the orientation of the bed according to Feng Shui?

When we are awake (yang) and working at a desk, we are activating our future and therefore we consider the forward direction of the desk as the most important direction, in front of whoever is sitting at it.

When we sleep, we must instead recover our energies (yin) and reconnect with our roots (past, origins), so the most important direction is the one behind, that is towards the nape (direction of the head of the bed). In some cases, in Feng Shui, we consider two directions (neck and feet), but these are advanced applications.

What the science says

Feng Shui - direction of the head of the bed. It was only a few years ago that science began to understand something about the phenomenon of "sleep". Until recently, in fact, the idea that the quality of sleep could be different according to the direction in which the body is oriented was simply derided on a scientific level (however, there was a clear reason for it). Instead, studies conducted in the United States of America in the 1970s and replicated in Europe a few decades later showed that sleeping with your head to the north increases the duration of REM sleep. REM sleep is the deepest one, considered important for the correct restoration of strength in the individual. However, this is a slight increase. Even sleeping with the head towards the east, there is an increase in REM sleep, which in this case is even more mild.

It would therefore seem that humans have cells that function as magnetoreceptors, as has been suspected for some time, also considering that, based on indirect indications, it seems that other mammals also have this ability (for example, cows and deer). The idea, therefore, that head-to-toe direction affects sleep seems to be increasingly plausible.

Sleeping with your head to the north

In fact, north-facing sleep seems to be the most restful of all. This is traditionally recommended in Europe. However, this sleep may be too restful, i.e. suitable for people who do very heavy physical work, such as bricklayer, carpenter, etc.

For people who do an office job, or a job that does not require a great deal of physical effort, the east direction seems preferable, which is always invigorating but leaves the mind more active and clearer.

The south and west directions, on the other hand, should be avoided.

Vastu and Feng Shui

How do they think in the East instead? According to the Vastu Shastra (an Indian discipline comparable to Feng Shui) the best direction for the head of the bed is the south. This is because the mind, which resides in the brain (head), is considered to be of negative polarity on a magnetic level, and therefore combines better with the positive south pole. Sleeping with your head to the north is considered unfavorable and a harbinger of difficulties in life. A vision diametrically opposite to the European one!

FENG SHUI: HOME DESIGN AND COLORS

The Vishnu Purana, considered one of the most important Hindu religious texts, states: "It is beneficial to rest with the head facing east or south. The man who falls asleep with his head positioned in opposite directions gets sick".

Head north or south?

As if that weren't enough, in 2009 Indian scientists and medical researchers carried out an experiment on sleep, using 40 women and asking them to take turns sleeping for 12 consecutive weeks in one of four geographic directions. This time, however, we did not study the quality of sleep but the effect that sleep could have on people. Different chemical and hormonal parameters were measured and the result - guess what! - was that the significantly better direction to sleep in is south, while north increases stress hormones. North would therefore be the worst direction to sleep in!

We can safely say that, at the moment, science is groping in the dark about it. As the literature on sleep and geographic directions is very sparse, science cannot help us.

How do you explain the difference between East and West?

In the west, it is usually recommended to sleep with your head north; in the east with the head to the south. How can this contradiction be explained?

Feng Shui bed head north

The simplest explanation is that it might be better for us to sleep with our head to the north, while for the Orientals it might be better to sleep with our heads to the south. Westerners, who tend to be more aggressive and with a higher level of testosterone, may prefer a deeper sleep while the less aggressive Orientals may increase the yang in their lives by sleeping with their head to the south.

In reality, there are many factors that influence sleep, so it is very difficult to identify which is the most important, also because certainly this varies from person to person, and for the same person, even from moment to moment in their life.

Furthermore, a distinction must be made between sleep quality and long-term sleep effect. Many times, it is not clear what you are talking about, and this too leads to confusion.

A step forward with Feng Shui

In Feng Shui, although the indications coming from oriental culture are generally respected, an important step forward is taken. In fact, we come to affirm that the favorable and unfavorable directions are personalized; more specifically, for a certain person some directions are more suitable for achieving certain outcomes in life, while others are less suitable.

The basic theories are limited to eight directions, but it is also possible to operate with 24 directions, indeed this is probably the division that has the greatest effect. Furthermore, in Feng Shui (and in Chinese astrology, the Ba Zi, a powerful analysis tool to be integrated with Feng Shui) the idea is accepted that, in different periods of life, we may need to change the orientation of the bed.

From our experience, this seems to us the most logical position and the most confirmed by the experimental data. So let's see the point of view of Feng Shui.

How does the bed affect us, according to Feng Shui?

Feng Shui bed arrangement. The decidedly prevalent activity that we carry out in the room is rest, the recovery of strength, the regeneration of the body and mind, the accumulation of energy to face an important task. And for women, even conception and pregnancy, which require a lot of energy. So, in Feng Shui sleep affects everything related to health, family, intimacy and private life.

FENG SHUI: HOME DESIGN AND COLORS

So, it is a bit illusory to think that you are pointing your bed in the personal direction of 'success' or 'money', and to have a big effect! Just as, conversely, it is ridiculous to think that the orientation of the desk (which we use in a waking state) affects our sleep and related activities.

Of course, it is possible to orient the bed in a direction related to money or success, calculated with Feng Shui, but at this point - since there is already a contradiction in use, and since money and success are not used while you sleep - if you really want to use the bed to pursue these ends (the desk is much more important), you need to use the forward orientation (of the feet). Money and success, in fact, concern the external, social, public life of the person.

Precisely for these reasons, from now on in this article we focus instead on the use of the headboard direction for health, regeneration, family, and the possibility of becoming pregnant: all reserved activities and yin, according to Feng Shui.

THE FAVORABLE AND UNFAVORABLE PERSONAL DIRECTIONS AND THE EIGHT PALACES METHOD

Before proceeding, we must quickly examine the well-known '8 personal directions' (favorable and unfavorable). I say 'well known' because anyone who is interested a little in Feng Shui, sooner or later encounters this theory, which historically derives from a Feng Shui method developed and made public about 4-5 centuries ago: the Ba Zhai or "Method of 8 Palaces" (or "Method of the 8 Houses"). Subsequently, simplifications were drawn from this method (such as the 8 favorable and unfavorable directions, the east / west house method, etc.).

There are strong chances that the method itself (I am referring to the original Ba Zhai) is incorrect or incomplete, or even that it is an incorrect Feng Shui text created specifically to confuse enemies, on the orders of an ancient emperor of China. But let's leave this aside momentarily until we have historical certainty about it.

8 directions, Ming Gua and Feng Shui

In the Feng Shui Method of the 8 Houses, people are classified into 8 types (associated with the numbers from 1 to 9 - excluding the number 5 - and the corresponding trigrams), based on the year of birth. The number associated with a person is called the Kua (or Gua, or Kwa) or Ming Gua number (later we will publish a detailed article on the calculation of the Ming Gua).

Each Gua number has 4 favorable and 4 unfavorable directions associated with it; however, the eight qualities of energy can be listed from the most unfavorable to the most favorable, as I have done below. The 8 qualities, associated in Feng Shui from time to time to the 8 directions according to the Ming Gua, are:

SHENG QI: Regenerating Breath (generally considered very favorable)

YEN NIEN: Long Life (very favorable)

TIEN YI: Heavenly Doctor (favorable)

FU WEI: (Hidden Position) - Direction of Life (neutral)

HUO HAI: Accidents and Bad Luck (slightly unfavorable)

LIU SHA: Six Curses (unfavorable)

WU KWEI: Five Ghosts (very unfavorable)

CHUEH MING: Total Loss, Catastrophe (very unfavorable)

Is good direction really always good?

As we know, in Feng Shui there are no concepts of right / wrong and good / bad, but only of appropriate / inappropriate. Therefore, to give an example, even if in general Sheng Qi is considered favorable, for some objectives it is inadequate and can have negative effects; conversely, Liu Sha is considered unfavorable but can instead be very good for some particular activities or situations.

In our case, speaking of the bed and private (non-working) life, for simplicity we will always refer to the list above.

How to use favorable and unfavorable Feng Shui directions

Let's now look at an example. Sheng Qi has revitalizing abilities, it attracts the new and favors changes, studies and new departures. If a woman wants to conceive, she can use the Sheng Qi direction as the head of the bed orientation. As well as if he wants to recover his strength, or strengthen the health of a person in convalescence.

If, on the other hand, the Sheng Qi direction is used not as a head but 'towards the feet', it influences the active, external life. This could favor changes and novelties at work or in relationships, but as already mentioned this outcome is unlikely as from the point of view of Feng Shui the bed (and sleep) are very little connected to work.

However, you can use the Sheng Qi front direction when placing a work desk, and this will affect your work activity (and little or no sleep).

How to activate a direction with Feng Shui

This is the little Feng Shui secret that I want to share in this article ... it is not enough to orient the bed (or any other fixed position) in a certain direction: to work, the direction must be properly activated, with objects or symbols that recall the function and the goal you want to achieve.

Feng Shui - sleep well, head north. To activate a direction, in professional Feng Shui the Date Selection is used, that is, an ideal date and time are calculated to activate the direction. This is quite a strong activation, but it must be done using at least 24 spatial directions and 22 temporal archetypes. Of course, first you need to know which direction to activate and if it can be activated: and this can only be said by Chinese astrology (Ba Zi, commonly translated as "Four Pillars of Destiny", the highest level of personalization) and Feng Shui.

If, on the other hand, you just turn the bed in one of the favorable directions when it happens, you must be lucky enough to do so on a neutral or at least not unfavorable date and time (which is not so unlikely), and activate the direction with a symbol, a decoration, a piece of furniture or an appropriate object. Precisely for this reason, moving the bed or desk according to the rules of Feng Shui does not always work well. The 'time' factor is decisive: the archetypes that are dominating at that moment at the temporal level may not agree on the activation of the direction.

How to use the 8 favorable and unfavorable directions practically.

If there is a choice between multiple directions, Feng Shui recommends choosing the most favorable one.

If the bed cannot be moved and the direction is good, neutral or slightly unfavorable, for Feng Shui there is no problem.

If the bed cannot be moved, and the orientation is in one of the worst two directions (Wu Kwei and Chueh Ming), a protective symbol can be used above the head of the bed (attention: it doesn't have to be something heavy or looming!), positioned with the intention of protecting.

Sleeping with the direction of the head to the north

Orientation and bed arrangement with Feng Shui. There is no Feng Shui book that indicates the need to sleep with your head to the north. After all, if everyone has personal favorable and unfavorable directions, which change according to the Ming Gua (annual personal Gua number), how can one think that the north is always a good direction for everyone? For some, the north will be associated with the most negative directions: Wu Kwai, or Chueh Ming ...

The idea that you must absolutely sleep with your head to the north is simply wrong and does not come from Feng Shui: there are equally good alternative directions and, in any case, not all those who sleep with their head to the north have a satisfactory sleep, and not all those who sleep with their heads to the south or west sleep badly. However, this idea has become a real diktat: years ago, I wrote an article in a well-known Italian magazine in which I dealt with this topic, clarifying that it is a false idea, and the editor felt compelled to correct me (without warning me, obviously)!

Generally, it is in the books of bio-architecture, radiesthesia or geobiology that "the rule of the head to the north" is reported, but despite the large number of texts that I have consulted, a credible reason for this statement is never given. The various hypotheses mentioned in the books (such as that of the alignment with the earth's magnetic field that would act on the hemoglobin of the blood, containing iron) are not valid because, in fact, they are only hypotheses and not confirmed theories.

Experiment on yourself

One piece of advice I would like to give to all people who travel is to note how you sleep when you change the direction of your head when sleeping. The same thing can be done on vacation or in informal and / or momentary situations in which it is possible to sleep in a different position from the one we have at home.

We must get to know ourselves: if we notice a particularly relaxing and different sleep from others, it is important to note the direction of the bed. To do this, just bring a small compass with you (an indispensable element for those interested in Feng Shui!) ... then we will try to replicate the orientation at home to see if it gives us the same effect or not.

Practical method for orienting the bed (direction of the headboard) according to Feng Shui.

We have seen that science cannot help us; we have seen that Feng Shui is a more advanced tool and offers us personalized guidelines. However, the effect of these directions is not yet certain from the experimental point of view;

moreover, for those who do not practice Feng Shui professionally it may be difficult to apply the method.

For this reason, we want to summarize what has been said in this article and provide some simple final indications on how to proceed to orient the headboard of your bed, using Feng Shui.

First of all, keep in mind that it is absolutely not mandatory to sleep with your head to the north; moreover, the position of the bedroom with respect to the entrance door and the position of the bed inside the room, according to authentic Feng Shui, definitely have priority over that of the orientation of the bed.

Never place the bed in an awkward, exposed or unpleasant position just to have your head in a certain direction, even if the direction is favorable!

Consider this: if the effects of a particular direction were clear-cut and incontrovertible, it is evident that we would all have known it for some time. If there is confusion and discord even among scientists, it means that the effects of direction are negligible compared to the other factors I have indicated above.

Still wanting to give some general indications, we can say that in Feng Shui the north, north west and north east directions are considered good and restful; East and South East are also fine and leave the mind more active and dynamic. The southern direction is very activating and not suitable for everyone. Southwest and west in general are not recommended, although they may be fine for some people. Each direction is associated with specific qualities of sleep.

Orientation of the head of the bed and eight directions: advantages and disadvantages

Headboard facing north: offers a deep and restorative sleep, is suitable for people who do heavy physical work and those suffering from insomnia, also good for children who have frequent nocturnal awakenings. If a person is already quiet, it can cause losses.

FENG SHUI: HOME DESIGN AND COLORS

Headboard facing north-east: a position that greatly activates the dream activity and nightmares. You can use it if you want to dream more and remember dreams. According to Feng Shui, it is not suitable for people who are mentally unstable or who are going through a period of psychological or emotional crisis.

Headboard facing east - a good direction for children and young people. East brings dynamism, development, optimism. It favors intellectual activity, studies and an active mind. Not recommended for people suffering from insomnia, anxiety or nerves.

Headboard facing south east: a better position than you think, suitable for young people, favors a peaceful and harmonious life.

Headboard facing south: according to Feng Shui, this is the most active point. Deep sleep is not encouraged. It can induce hyperactivity. It is suitable for very quiet, habitual or sleepy people. Not recommended for others.

Headboard facing south west: this direction can be very good for some and very annoying for others. This must be verified on a personal level.

Headboard facing west: this is the direction in which the sun goes down and strength is lost. It can cause laziness, indolence, inactivity. Increase the worries. Not bad for the elderly.

Headboard facing north-west: this is an important direction, more suitable for adults or the elderly. It gives a deep sleep and a feeling of security. It favors a peaceful and orderly life but does not favor falling asleep.

FENG SHUI: HOME DESIGN AND COLORS

COLORS ACCORDING TO THE PHILOSOPHY OF FENG- SHUI LIVING

Feng Shui is an ancient oriental discipline that combines philosophy and architecture, to furnish spaces so that positive energies are generated for the spirit and the body. The term Feng Shui refers to the concepts of wind and water, which represent health, happiness, peace and prosperity.

In the East, the principles of Feng Shui are not only applied to furniture, but also to the design of buildings and neighborhoods. In general, as regards interior design, it is possible to refer to some rules, which take into account the presence of magnetic and energy fields to choose the arrangement of the furnishings and give life to spaces that generate well-being and are comfortable for those who attends.

The meaning of colors

The choice of colors is very important for Feng Shui, each one has its own meaning and generates a series of emotions and sensations. In general, colors derive from yin-yang and its shades: the maximum of light is yang, the absence of light is yin, in the middle there are the colors as they are perceived by the human eye. Each color has its own type of energy, information that reaches our subconscious and influences it, even if we are unaware of it.

Let's see what each color is associated with in Feng Shui:

Green - Wood energy: it is the color of spring, liver and eyes. Where there is green there is vegetation and therefore water and food, essential for our survival. Our body associates the perception of green with the presence of plants. The more intense it is, the more favorable the environment is. It is used when it is necessary to transmit tranquility, relaxation, cooperation.

FENG SHUI: HOME DESIGN AND COLORS

Red, lilac, celestial - Fire energy: these are the colors of summer, heart and blood circulation. They are activating colors, so they should be used in moderation and in the environments where activities are carried out.

Yellow, brown, dull gray - Earth energy: these are the colors of late summer, stomach and touch. The shades more or less tending to the color of the earth make these colors become those of fertility, abundance and accumulation (fertile earth) or that of solidity and stability (earth rock).

White, silver, metallic - Metal energy: these are the colors of autumn and lungs. They favor inner research and tend to calm down.

Shades of blue - Water energy: these are the colors of winter, arenas, genitals, ears, instinct, intuition and dreams. Again, the hue leads more or less towards yin and yang. Dark shades are yin, light shades are yang. They are calming and introspective colors.

THE RIGHT COLOR FOR EVERY ROOM

Each room in the house for Feng Shui must have a color that best suits it, based on the functions we perform there.

Entrance: it is the place of passage between outside and inside the house. The ideal colors for Feng Shui are blue, green and pink with yang.

Living room: is the place of meeting and conviviality. For this area the bright tones of red and yellow are good as well as the colors closer to those of the earth, which return a feeling of welcome.

Kitchen: it is a stimulating and lively environment. The right color is yellow, combined with the colors of the earth.

Dining room: it is a convivial but relaxing room, so it is good to choose green, yellow, pink, earth tones.

FENG SHUI: HOME DESIGN AND COLORS

Bedroom: it is the place of relaxation and intimacy, therefore intense colors should be avoided, to switch to pastel shades of pink, green or cream.

Bathroom: it is an area where you spend a limited time, so you can use bright colors such as turquoise or red combined with white or black.

Children's room: it is an energizing room, which stimulates imagination and creativity. Red and orange are perfect for the play area, while turquoise or green are good for the bedroom and study area.

SIMPLE DIRECTIONS TO CHOOSE THE RIGHT COLOR!

Color in science and psychology

Colors and Feng Shui. The use of colors in Feng Shui is a topic that arouses a lot of interest, above all because it is through color that we provide a "personality" to individual premises. So let's examine this topic a little more in depth.

According to the scientific interpretation, the colors can be divided into primary (yellow, red and blue) and secondary, which derive from the combination of two primaries (for example, green = yellow plus blue; orange = red plus yellow, etc.).

Black is the absence of color, white the sum of all colors.

Finally, the colors that together give white are said to be complementary. For example, yellow and purple, or red and green. All this is very interesting but it does not directly concern the energetic interaction between color and the individual, and only partially the message that color transmits to our animal and / or unconscious part.

In this regard, many psychological, sociological and similar studies have been carried out.

FENG SHUI: HOME DESIGN AND COLORS

At the beginning of the 20th century, research was carried out to maximize the working time of workers and employees in companies. A case that has remained famous is that of acid yellow bathrooms: from experiments of various kinds, it has been seen that, on average, people tend to stay as little as possible in an environment of this color. Therefore, to reduce the time "lost" in the bathroom, this chromatic suggestion has been introduced. The same effect is also obtained with other shades such as the color "vomit".

It is one of the earliest examples in the West of the use of information introduced into the environment in a deliberate, but undeclared way, to influence people's behavior. The acid yellow color is associated, on an unconscious level, with an arid, inhospitable and poisoned land and it is therefore natural that the organism tries to get away as much as possible from this place. But be careful... this does not mean that in some cases it is not useful.

The results of scientific research mostly coincide with the information that we can find in Feng Shui or other traditions, so it is to these that we will refer from here on.

Generally speaking, colors derive from yin-yang polarity and its various manifestations.

At one extreme we have light, manifestation of the maximum yang; to the other the darkness, maximum yin.

In the middle are all the colors received by the human eye. Each color is associated with a type of energy, and subtle information, which is directly transmitted to the deep unconscious. So, let's examine the colors and their characteristics.

GREEN

Green in all its shades is associated with Wood energy, spring, liver and eyes. Our body associates the perception of green with the presence of plants. Where there is a lot of green there is a lot of water (vital for animals); moreover, it is easy to get food, either directly from plants or from animals housed in woods or forests.

FENG SHUI: HOME DESIGN AND COLORS

The more the greenery is luxuriant and strong, the more we are certain of being in a favorable and rich environment. Green therefore favors tranquility, relaxation, cooperation, social relations and friendship. In fact, where there is an abundance of food, there is no need to compete with other animals (or with individuals of the same species) to obtain it.

RED

Red, lilac, violet, magenta in all their shades, and light blue are considered to be colors of Fire, associated with summer, the heart and blood circulation. They are very active and activating colors. Celestial is the color of the sky when the sun shines, and is therefore considered the color of Fire par excellence. Red is the second strongest. They are connected to activity, stimulation, reactivity and alertness of mind, learning, mental activity. You need to know how to dose these colors; since they are very activating it is better not to overdo it. Red sometimes takes on dangerous characteristics (blood flow); think of the signs...

Sometimes red is also combined with forms of Fire: the triangular signs are proof of very ancient energetic and genetic connections, which go beyond any cultural difference.

Feng Shui is not "a Chinese bio-architecture", or a fashion, which we must strive to learn; but it is something deep and inherent to all human beings, who share the same energetic structure. More than "learning" Feng Shui, in fact, we must try to "find" it within ourselves. Feng Shui is a heritage of humanity, a knowledge shared by all cultures, even the ancient Western tradition. Many names, one substance.

YELLOW AND BROWN

Yellow, brown, dull gray with all its shades, terracotta color, are considered Earth colors, associated with late summer (when fruits and crops are harvested), stomach, touch.

FENG SHUI: HOME DESIGN AND COLORS

If the color resembles the crushed, fertile earth, it is more yin; if it gives the impression of rock, it is more yang. Earth yin is associated with maturation, fertility, abundance, accumulation; Earth yang to solidity and stability.

WHITE

White, the color silver and in general "metallic" gray are associated with the Metal energy, with autumn, with the lungs. They are colors that encourage introspection and lead inward. Generally, they are cold, they tend to calm down, to quiet down. White is great in a room used for meditation.

THE BLUE TONES

The transparent, the glaucous, the opaque glass, the cold blue and the sea-green, the blue and the black are colors of water. The darker the color, the more we are towards the yin form of the Water energy. These too are typically calming colors and lead inward. They are related to winter, the kidneys and genitals, ears, instinct, intuition and dreams.

THE EFFECTS OF COLOR

As we have already been able to guess from the descriptions made above, a color can come in various "forms". Also, a color can come in a solid color or not. The solid color is more yin and tends to lead inward. If, on the other hand, the color is "moved", it has a more yang or movement characteristic. If the color is faded, this is reminiscent of a vast landscape with splashes of color (objects farther away are seen "faded") and introduces some depth.

A color can be bright (more yang) or opaque (more yin), active or neutral, embossed or smooth, solid or wavy (scratched, sponged, torn, brushed, drawn, dotted ...), bright or dark, and so on.

Each of these features provides a particular "personality" to a painted wall.

FENG SHUI: HOME DESIGN AND COLORS

COLORS IN SPATIAL PERCEPTION

Finally, there are the color combinations. It is quite rare, in fact, that there is only one color in a room, even in the furnishings; and it is not even desirable.

Typically, we will have four large splashes of color: the floor, the walls, the furniture and the ceiling. Following what we see in nature, a room for yang activity should have the floor darker than the walls and the walls darker than the ceiling (in nature the ground is usually darker than what is at eye level, which in turn is darker than the open sky above us). In a more yin activity room, however, things can also be set up differently.

How to choose a color according to Feng Shui

When choosing the color for a room, five pieces of information must first be taken into account:

- the orientation of the house
- the area of the house where the room is located
- the function of the room
- the energy characteristics of the person / s who will occupy that room
- the aesthetic sensitivity of the person.

Trust your instinct

From the interrelation of these five points, a "rose" of selected colors will be formed, from which to choose the final one, based on the preferences of the occupants.

I get a lot of requests from people asking me for color advice, but it seems clear to me that giving general advice is useless, and can even be harmful. If you don't know the subject, follow your instincts: it's the best thing. Throw away the suggestions that are now in all the magazines. Learn to listen to yourself.

Beware of false 'Feng Shui rules'!

FENG SHUI: HOME DESIGN AND COLORS

Saying that "green is good for the kitchen" or that "in the west you need to use white, in the southwest you need to use yellow" or "red (or black) is used to treat depression" are generic statements that can be misleading.

What kind of green? Is it suitable for room lighting? Is it suitable for me? What if green is the worst possible information for my unconscious? And how much green should I put on?

And again: do I have to wear red? Or should I paint my room red? Or again: do I have to take a red stone with me?

The categorical statements of this type derive from the misunderstanding of the Bagua (or Pa Kua), a pattern of 3 × 3 boxes or ' domicilii'. This diagram shows the color associated with each direction and energy phase (for example: south-Fire-red). But this in no way implies that red should be used in the south, nor that it should be used exclusively in the south! These statements are incorrect, and followed to the letter can be harmful to some. They have nothing to do with authentic Feng Shui.

FENG SHUI: HOME DESIGN AND COLORS

HOW TO FURNISH A LIVING ROOM IN FENG SHUI STYLE: PRACTICAL TIPS TO FOLLOW

Furnishing the Feng Shui living room is possible, just follow some practical tips to create a harmonious living room full of positive energy. So, if you want a perfect home layout for Feng Shui, you've come to the ideal place, because today we will reveal all the secrets to give harmony and well-being to your most cherished rooms, for a welcoming and warm home.

Here are some practical tips to follow on how to furnish a living room in Feng Shui style. Feng Shui is an ancient discipline of Chinese origin which literally means "Wind" and "Water", bearers of joy, peace and serenity. Feng Shui aims to create a welcoming and hospitable environment within the home by seeking naturalness and a flow of positive energies. So, if you are looking for hints and ideas on how to furnish the living room, here are the practical tips to follow to furnish a living room in Feng Shui style.

The living room according to Feng Shui is the room in the house where you can relax in company or alone. To furnish a living room in Feng Shui style, the first thing to consider is the shape, that must be rectangular or square, with a high ceiling. Exposed beams are to be avoided, as they are carriers of negative energies.

The sofa must be positioned facing the entrance door so that those who enter will immediately feel welcome in a hospitable and warm environment. The backrest should be placed close to the wall to give a sense of protection and safety to those who sit. Also avoid placing it near doors and windows to avoid drafts. The path from the entrance to the sofa must be well defined to prevent those who enter from feeling uncomfortable and lost.

Warm colors and white furniture that let natural light filter through.

The furniture of a Feng Shui style living room will be arranged in such a way as to allow freedom of movement and should not prevent natural light from entering the home. To furnish a living room in Feng Shui style, pay attention to the corners of the room, considered carriers of negative energies: they will be personalized with a green plant or a lamp with a warm light.

Near the sofa and armchairs will be placed a coffee table with a round shape that recalls the symbol of the sky. The fireplace will help to make the atmosphere welcoming and familiar if placed along a wall, never in the center of the room.

Walls colored green, a color of balance and relaxing according to Feng Shui.

Here are some tips on how to choose the color of the living room walls according to Feng Shui. In fact, colors also play a fundamental role in furnishing a living room in Feng Shui style. Lilac is the color to be preferred as it invites conviviality. Red is to be used carefully; if used in an exaggerated way it can trigger anger and agitation. White, associated with pastel colors, is perfect for all environments: it indicates determination and is extremely bright. Green is the color of balance, it recalls nature, it is relaxing and pleasant: the lighter and more subdued nuances are preferred.

Fire red walls for a Feng Shui living room.

The choice of colors according to Feng Shui is really important, as it is through these that we give character and harmony to the environment.

But what are the right colors for the living room according to Feng Shui? It is easy to say; first of all we must remember that according to the Chinese discipline, each color is associated with a type of energy.

As for the living room, it is possible to choose between different shades, such as green, synonymous with nature, harmony, tranquility and well-being; or, to furnish the Feng Shui living room, you can opt for yellow, synonymous with stability and solidity; white is also an excellent choice, because it is a symbol of peace and relaxation, as well as blue in all its shades.

HOW TO ARRANGE THE PICTURES THE FENG SHUI WAY IN THE LIVING ROOM

Arrange the paintings in line with the rest of the furniture, to keep the rooms harmonious.

FENG SHUI: HOME DESIGN AND COLORS

According to Feng Shui it is possible to furnish the living room with paintings and artistic works, the important thing is to choose naturalistic subjects and in shades close to the rest of the furniture.

Choosing subjects linked to nature is important to recreate a feeling of well-being and peace; to avoid too graphic and geometric designs, or disturbing subjects.

Furthermore, according to the Chinese discipline it is better to choose paintings with anti-reflective glass and neutral frames; in addition, it is important to arrange the images you like best in correspondence with your view.

Finally, if you decide to hang more paintings it is better to choose them of the same size and arrange them following a logical sense and, above all, at the same height so as not to create imbalances.

Now that you know all the techniques to furnish the living room in Feng Shui style, you just have to get to work and bring more harmony and well-being to your home.

FENG SHUI: HOME DESIGN AND COLORS

FENG SHUI TALISMANS AND AMULETS

Skeptics consider talismans to be an echo of paganism, which is best left in the past. In the old days, people attached a lot of importance to the magical amulet, but even today they can be useful if you choose them correctly and use them correctly. If our ancestors believed that a number of spells could influence success, today it is necessary not to hang up all kinds of amulets from esoteric shops.

It is enough to carefully analyze your life, understand what you are missing, what you should be striving for, and prioritize correctly. In addition, the choice of talismans is not easy, you need to know what the amulets are intended for, how they work, otherwise it can only make the situation worse.

Talismans, amulets, feng shui symbols have a different meaning and embodiment. There are focused amulets, there are those that have a wider functionality. However, each symbolic statuette or other talisman has its own meaning, and it is necessary to focus attention on it when choosing. Regardless of what you want to change in life. You need to start by defining your goal, which will determine the direction. The choice of the thematic mascot depends on it.

Buy the first pendant you like, if you want to buy a general-purpose talisman. This option is great as a gift. Each multifunctional symbol, as a rule, works to attract luck, success and happiness in the general sense of these words.

Which is suitable?

Each talisman has its own description, which contains all the information about its magical properties. From it you can find out whether this or that amulet is suitable for your purposes. It is not necessary to have serious problems, disasters and negative accidents to start working with feng shui talismans. Even if everything is fine in life, there are always aspects that need to be improved, or simply to maintain what you have already achieved. It is not enough to attract good luck, but it must also be kept. Guardian characters here will be more effective and useful.

FENG SHUI: HOME DESIGN AND COLORS

If the problem or goal is determined clearly enough, then you need to choose a specific amulet for the situation. Not enough money - symbols of abundance will help. Health problems - consider this particular category of talismans. Many amulets work to protect the home, the incentive to learn.

You can pick up and regulate the situation with loneliness, childbirth and health, career problems, if you choose the right amulet and activate its energy.

How to choose?

So, before choosing a talisman, you need to determine the direction in which it should work, and find out what it means. Chinese amulets are very common, finding and buying them is not difficult. Specialized esoteric shops offer us the famous "music of the wind" figurines: owls, three elders, golden pyramids, bells, snails. The most popular amulets that work with health, abundance, family well-being, career.

FOR HEALTH AND LONGEVITY

This is one of the current categories, especially since Eastern residents are famous for their longevity. The secret of this combines their lifestyle, harmony and faith in the magical talismans, which help to find peace, and to get along with themselves and others, and strengthens health.

Here are the most popular feng shui talismans for health.

Heron. It means long life, it symbolizes change for the better. Make sure you have such a bird in the house if you want to strengthen the spiritual and physical health of the family. This symbol has an excellent effect on the mental state of a person, calms the nerves, protects from stress, depression. Positive effect on the situation in the family, strengthens family ties, revives tradition.

Bamboo. This vegetation symbolizes not only determination, but also long life, as well as body strength. It is capable of providing resistance. Bamboo can be safely placed in the house, for example, on the walls. It works great as a guardian against the flow of negative energy from the outside. In the house, it will provide a favorable calm atmosphere. The health of family members will certainly improve.

Crane. These birds are very revered in China, in almost every house there is an image in the form of a painting or a statuette. This is a symbol of good health, long active life, abundance, a stable family.

It is necessary to know that only a pair of cranes works in this quality; individually, these birds are powerless.

Gourd. This traditional drinking vessel means a long healthy life, high libido. It is recommended to improve performance and love potential, regardless of gender, to strengthen family bonds. You can place yourself at the patient's bedside until complete recovery, and then activate the talisman again.

FOR WEALTH AND PROSPERITY

It is very important not only to choose the amulet that attracts cash flow, but also to place it in the right place, and to properly care for it.

Also, if you want to attract wealth into the house, work in the area located in the Southeast, which is responsible for this direction. In the wealth sector there should be no garbage, confusion of useless things, dirt, dust.

These amulets should be purchased if you want to get rich.

Cloth. To attract money, this attribute is acquired quite often. The red fabric, embroidered with gold flowers, screams of wealth. A variety of ornaments, patterns, hieroglyphs, talisman money images are embroidered as drawings. Such an attribute is placed in a prominent place, for example, and you can put a statuette with a similar object on top of it on the shelf.

Fish. The symbol of wealth, well-being, prosperity. Very powerful amulet, which works to attract financial flows. This attribute guarantees good news, abundance in the house and positive energy in it. By the way, live fish in an aquarium, according to Feng Shui, are also able to play the role of a talisman.

FENG SHUI: HOME DESIGN AND COLORS

Choose goldfish and place them in the southeast, carefully take care of the aquarium and the result is not long in coming.

The fountain. Water, according to Feng Shui, is endowed with tremendous power, so fountains are able to purify space and attract success, wealth. It is very important to properly care for the fountain so that the water does not stagnate.

Pot-bellied God. Most often, a smiling god carries a bag with him, from which, like a full horn, gifts of fate are poured out on a person. A great way to activate a pot-bellied god is to rub his belly exactly 40 times. At the same time, you need to focus on your financial dreams and only think about them. The patron saint of traders and those whose life depends on luck will surely help!

Money tree. Another powerful amulet that can be made in a symbolic incarnation, hung with real coins. Make sure you bury three coins in the ground, and don't take sprouts from poor people. Then it's better to buy it in a flower shop.

Toad. In his mouth he holds a coin, it symbolizes prosperity, prosperity, success. In addition to the wealth sector, you can put a toad in front of the entrance to the house, only he should look into the apartment. Required attributes: a removable coin in the mouth and a holder made of money.

Hieroglyph "Wealth". It can be applied independently with red paint on the door. It is believed that this sign will not only attract money, but also make the character of the householder better.

Bowl of Wealth. An effective symbol that activates cash flows, attracting them to the house where it is located. To make the house a full bowl, periodically arrange coins or sweets.

FENG SHUI: HOME DESIGN AND COLORS

FOR THE WELL-BEING OF THE FAMILY

The Chinese highly appreciate amulets that protect the family from negative energy, discord, conflict.

Butterflies. Embrace love, joy, light, lightness and harmony. The house in which these talismans are, will not only be strong, but also happy. Symbol of passion, romance, bright love.

Dragonfly. It maintains an atmosphere of ease, celebration, romance, creativity. It is recommended to place it in the bedroom, as it has a positive effect on libido.

Flamingo. It allows you to fulfill all the desires that are in the field of personal relationships. A joyful and happy talisman for love.

Dog Fu. This is one of the most powerful talismans that can save your family from any quarrel. The dog consists of two heterosexual lions. Choose the figurines of a benevolent appearance, smiling. If it is possible to put talismans outside the house, you can put Fu's angry dogs near it.

Cao Wan. The god of the family, rather severe, with his formidable air, does not give the possibility to disturb relations and problems from the outside. Constantly monitors family members and directs their behavior into the mainstream of harmony.

An elephant. This is a symbol of the family, which is not afraid of any obstacles, if you have such a talisman, the relationship is under serious protection. Purchase a new elephant after each holiday and provide a free shelf for this arrangement.

Carp. This symbol is extremely popular, it is good to give to newlyweds, because it attracts harmony, happiness in a relationship. This symbol has powerful energy, it symbolizes finality, which allows you to easily overcome obstacles.

Red lanterns. No wonder they throw lanterns on their wedding day, this beautiful tradition arose due to the ability of Chinese lanterns to save people from loneliness, find a mate, strengthen marriage.

FENG SHUI: HOME DESIGN AND COLORS

FOR CAREER AND GOOD LUCK

The following symbols are considered optimal talismans in this area:

horse - a brave, industrious, active animal, aspiring to the front, will perfectly assist in matters of going to the top;

ship - a very strong amulet, which attracts success in the financial sphere of life, regularly fill the boat with coins, so it will work even more actively;

dragon - a wise and harmonious symbol that can change the material state for the better;

pig - a symbol of fertility, including in professional and monetary areas, a piggy bank on the desktop is sure to bring good luck in business;

peacock - attracts fame and beauty, will ensure success in work, rise to the top.

Wind music

This amulet is able to level the flow of negative energy and to regulate the inhabitants of the house in a favorable way. To choose the right wind music for your home you need to know the following nuances:

- the amulet with five tubes attracts positive energy and prosperity;
- eight pipes mean well-being, attracts success;
- it is desirable that the pipes be hollow for the active circulation of energy;
- pipes are able to fill the house with positive energy and reduce the negative, so if the house has unfavorable zones, the wind music will increase the level of good energy in them;

FENG SHUI: HOME DESIGN AND COLORS

- narrow or uncomfortable corridors, dead ends, sharp corners, improper location of the bathroom, in the sewers from which good energy flows - a reason to put the music of the wind;
- if the view from the window is an unfavorable picture - the corner of the house, the garbage cans, the trees standing alone, the power poles, the wind music should be placed in the window;
- the maximum size of pipes for the house - 9 cm;
- avoid positioning over the head, above the bed;
- the tubes or bells should ring, so it is good that people can move them by pulling curtains or from gusts of wind from an open window;
- Before buying this talisman, carefully listen to its sound, you should like the tone, be discreet;
- The height of the placement should be such that you do not touch the amulet with your head while walking under it.

WHERE TO PUT THEM?

In order for talismans to work effectively, you need to place them correctly. To do this, divide your house into action zones and place the amulets in the appropriate part:

- the southeast is responsible for wealth, abundance;
- south for reputation and fame;
- southwest - for romance, love, passion;
- west - for children and creativity;
- east - for development, health;
- to the northeast - for learning, cognition;
- north: for career growth;
- northwest - to attract assistants.

Talisman amulets can be placed in front of the entrance, on the windowsill, thereby smoothing the sharp edges of the house. Put romantic symbols near the bed. Your desktop or your child's is a great platform for symbols of knowledge, career.

FENG SHUI: HOME DESIGN AND COLORS

BAGUA MAP AND FENG SHUI

Each house is a "small universe"

Feng Shui can truly improve our living conditions by simply creating an environment in harmony with the laws of nature.

Feng Shui is an ancient Chinese discipline that has its roots in the Taoist culture, of which it takes up two basic cosmological theories: the theory of Yin and Yang and the Theory of the five elements.

Approaching the art of Feng Shui therefore means preparing oneself at a level of perception of knowledge, forms, symbols and calculations aimed at searching for the sacred harmony existing between the human being and the universe in order to define those existing between the man and the place where he lives.

ART, PHILOSOPHY OR SCIENCE?

We can define Feng Shui as the expression of aesthetic rules inspired by principles of dynamics, thermodynamics and electromagnetism in order to harmonize the individual with the surrounding environment in order to improve their living conditions.

Quantum physics has shown us a reality that is anything but physical: matter is but an illusion! Everything in the universe is composed of energy: vortices of energy that vibrate constantly and with a specific characteristic sign: a particular vibration, measurable both in frequency and in intensity.

Each individual therefore has his own personal and unique vibratory frequency that distinguishes him. Living in a social dimension we are constantly interacting in a vibrational dimension of multi-frequencies.

FENG SHUI: HOME DESIGN AND COLORS

Any incompatible vibratory frequency makes maintaining one's energy balance a difficult and tiring process. On the contrary, the contact with similar vibratory sources allows the vital energy present in each individual (the Chi) to flow in a spontaneous and balanced way.

The Chi is also affected by the distribution and shape of the spaces. Therefore, the structural elements will take on importance inside a house, such as stairs, fireplaces, heating systems; furnishings like furniture, mirrors, curtains, plants, ornamental paintings; the position of doors, windows and dividing walls.

The Bagua

Feng Shui believes that, in the harmonic structure of an environment, the excess or lack of a single element can affect the energy of the whole house. One of the main sources of stress and anxiety, for example, is due to the excessive use of white and the lack of decorations on the walls.

By improving the environment, we live in, we will consequently improve the quality of our life.

To determine these harmonic correspondences, Feng Shui uses the "Bagua", a geomantic map inspired by the principles of the I Ching and the "Lo Shu" square, which makes each room in the house correspond to a specific aspect of life: career, relationships social, children, marriage, fame, wealth, family, acquaintance, associating it with a cardinal direction and a trigram, according to an octagonal scheme.

The eight forces of the trigrams

Each of the trigrams consists of three lines, in eight different combinations.

The combinations represent the eight forces generated by the cosmic interaction of the five elements: Fire, Earth, Metal, Water and Wood. Legend has it that, around 2088 BC, after a disastrous flood, a turtle sent by the river god emerged from the Lo river. The turtle had drawn on its shell a magic square inside which the numbers from 1 to 9 were inscribed, so that the sum of the

FENG SHUI: HOME DESIGN AND COLORS

numbers presents in each row, in each column and in both diagonals of the table in which they were written, always gave the same number: 15, a number also known as a magic constant or magical constant, of great importance in Chinese tradition.

Each trigram has a precise meaning. They are figures made up of three horizontal lines placed one above the other and combined with each other in eight different ways. The lines that make up each trigram are of two types: whole, representing the positive polarity, Yang; and broken, representing the negative polarity, Yin.

Each section of the Bagua is characterized by a number and a keyword that represents a specific relational and emotional area of life:

Water trigram is Yang. It represents: freedom, flow, new stories, beginnings. Connected to the North.

Trigram of the Earth is Yin and represents the ability to receive, to welcome, to grow and to fulfill. Connected to the South West.

Thunder trigram is Yang and represents decision and movement. It is the symbol of growth and movement. External influences, family, intrusions. Connected to the East.

Wind trigram is Yin and represents indecision and pain, rules, scents. Its characteristic is the capacity of extension characteristic of the growth of plants in spring. Harmony, happiness, negotiations, progress. Connected to the South East.

Center. The central area of the square, represents unity and completeness. It represents the heart of the house, of relationships, our essence.

Sky Trigram is Yang and represents strength, authority and solidity. Give and take, emotional support, friendships. Connected to the North West.

Trigram of the Lake is Yin represents love, joy and gladness. Creative love, sexuality, sensuality, arousal. Connected to the West.

FENG SHUI: HOME DESIGN AND COLORS

The Mountain Trigram is Yang and represents stillness, endurance and solidity. It is related to sitting and meditation. Communication, awareness of oneself and others. Connected to the North East.

Fire trigram is Yin. It depicts elegance, intelligence, clarity and accomplishment. Connected to the South.

HOW TO USE THE BAGUA MAP

The bagua map is superimposed on the floor plan of the house, making the "Center" of the octagon coincide with the center of the floor plan of the house, making sure that the entry point coincides with the water gully.

The ideal condition would be the exact correspondence between the position of each room with the gua of the map: the office in the prosperity area, the bedroom in the creative love area and so on. In reality it is quite rare that such a correspondence occurs, especially here in the West.

But don't worry, we will not be forced to move to improve our domestic harmony. It will be sufficient to introduce some new object, eliminate some others, move some furniture and only in case of extreme necessity remove some walls, to facilitate the flow of Chi and create balance and harmony in the environment in which we live, obtaining a considerable change in conditions of daily life.

The first thing to do is to carefully observe the objects around us: those we perceive to have negative energy we will throw away without any hesitation. We will reposition the remaining ones correctly, placing them in the symbolically relevant areas: for example, the photo of your wife in the love area.

It is also very important that there are no areas of the house that are untidy or dirty.

FENG SHUI: HOME DESIGN AND COLORS

Particular attention must also be paid to the bathroom: the toilet must always be kept closed, so as not to waste vital energy.

FENG SHUI: THE BAGUA MAP TO DISTINGUISH ENVIRONMENTS

Do you want a home in peace and harmony? Feng Shui can help you. This time we will talk about the Bagua map, so grab a pen and paper.

We have already talked a lot about Feng Shui and we promise to keep doing it. We love this style and we know how useful it is to harmonize environments and make them much more comfortable.

This age-old philosophy is full of wisdom and invites us to use energy to our advantage. For this reason, decoration plays a fundamental role.

To achieve its harmonic goals, Feng Shui uses many tools. In particular, there is a fundamental one, on which everything else is based. Indeed, without it, it would be difficult to make a complete study and understand Feng Shui: we are talking about the Bagua map.

What is the Bagua Map of Feng Shui?

Through the Bagua Map of Feng Shui we can distribute the energies present in our home, relating each space to a fundamental aspect of our life.

The Bagua map divides the house into nine areas in which five elements, shapes, materials, colors and even yin and yang intervene. It is a model that can be applied to any space, whether in a home or an office, but also in a single room.

How to draw a Bagua map?

Feng Shui uses this map as the main tool to manifest its theories. If we are in front of the front door, we must draw a straight horizontal line from one side to the other and, starting from there, divide the house into nine equal parts.

FENG SHUI: HOME DESIGN AND COLORS

At the door we will always find one of the areas at the bottom of our map: knowledge and culture, career and profession, travel and friends. From there we will know which area the other rooms in the house are connected to.

The nine areas of the Bagua map and their meaning

These are the areas in which Feng Shui divides spaces:

1. Prosperity and wealth

This area is linked to luck and wealth, the element that represents it the most is wood. Its colors are red, purple and blue. Be careful if your wealth zone is in the bathroom, as you could suffer economic losses. If so, everything has a solution: always lower the toilet lid and put some plants with drooping leaves to attract prosperity.

2. Fame and reputation on the Bagua map

In this area lies what we want to become, our desires and what we would like to project outwardly. To enhance it, use red, pink or purple. Its element is fire, so candles should never be missing.

3. Love and marriage

This area of the house is connected, not only with the love of a couple, but also with the way we relate to others. The bond with the mother plays a very important role here, but also with nature. So its colors are the shades of the earth. In addition, the decoration of this zone should be even: two chandeliers, two bedside tables, two vases, etc.

4. Health and family

The green color and wood are its representatives, which lead us towards the discovery of our roots. According to Feng Shui experts, if there are unresolved situations in our life in the past, it will be difficult for us to move forward and consolidate new projects.

5. Creativity and children

The dominant material of this area of the Bagua map must be metal and pastel shades and white. It is linked to our ability to give life to projects, to give life to everything we have in mind from start to finish.

6. Knowledge and culture in the Bagua map

In this area you will find self-love. It is the place on the Bagua map in which to find peace and serenity, in which to reflect and deepen self-knowledge.

Its colors are blue, green and black. As for decoration, you will have to use soft, warm and harmonious materials, which invite you to relax. As for the lighting, however, it must be soft and indirect.

7. Career and profession

Here is the area of the house dedicated to our profession, which also translates into the way we show ourselves to the world and in social relationships. If you want more clarity in this sense, use dark colors, aqua and organic shapes. Natural plants are essential here.

8. Travel and friends

In this area we find the center of our personal growth, the recognition of the role of those who are part of our journey. We must use travel photos, memories of the places that have filled us with happiness. As for colors, white, black and gray are the most suitable.

9. Center

In the center of the Bagua map is a fixed, motionless area. Here order is essential, according to Feng Shui theories. For this reason, it will be necessary to place a crystal ball with the task of keeping all the energies in balance.

Now that you know what the Feng Shui map consists of and how it distributes the energies in each area of your home, we invite you to follow our tips for decorating and harmonizing spaces.

FENG SHUI: HOME DESIGN AND COLORS

FENG SHUI AND BIOARCHITECTURE

The interior of San Gottardo, 8, in Milan has two courtyards: the first is classical, the second, almost hidden, looks like a doorway to the past, a courtyard that seems to bring you back to contact with the earth and nature, where we meet 'Materia Vera'. A huge Newfoundland greets me and a trail of cats escort me up to the wooden stairs that lead me to the room used for the event I went to for you, last May 26: The Conference on Feng Shui and bio-architecture - a combined approach for harmony of living spaces.

Materia Vera is an architecture and bio-architecture studio. And already from the frame that welcomes you, you realize that it is a particular study: it is in fact a landscape design in an ecological key.

While waiting for all the reserved seats to fill up, I savor the smells and perfumes emanating from the studio. Wood in the first place. Fruit in the background: the dyes on my side are strictly natural, based on pure natural pigments.

I met Feng Shui by chance, helping to renovate a friend's house. Struck by the impact and validity of the applications of Chinese theory, she gave up the genetics of psychiatric diseases to devote herself entirely to what is defined as the "home body" - that is, that interrelation of man with the places where he lives - the western scientific approach is optimal with the eastern energy-intuitive one. "Each of us instinctively knows how he is in his space and tries to arrange it as best as possible, but sometimes we block ourselves by creating spaces that are not suited to us".

But what is Feng Shui? A discipline that is actually much older than the arbitrary XXVI century BC of which someone speaks, the first signs of it appear already in Neolithic China, even 4500 years before Christ: sacred places positioned in certain points according to the constellations, acupuncture centers in places geopathically capable of absorbing energies to the maximum. Why shouldn't we do it too in our own small way? How? Simple, by connecting the areas of the house with the parts of our body and of our family through that Bagua grid which, on the basis of the 8 sectors (the classic cardinal and secondary signs) will apply not only to our home - after having simply established which is the front and the back, as in a person, the light, the noises, the materials will be associated with each place that is most suitable - but also with those who fill it: our family unit. "The conformation of the natural environment, the shapes and positions of the built structures, the way in which each body-house is placed in relation to the macrocosm and receives light, air, energy, condition the quality of life of the inhabitants."

Let's open the doors of this world not so well known to everyone - I must admit that I didn't know it! - talking about the key characters of what is the house par excellence: the father, the mother, the sons, the daughters. Parents represent the poles of the house, Yin and Yang, because they start everything else. Without them there would be no family, there would be no home. And serenity depends on them. They are the male and female parts, which nevertheless each one has in himself and that everyone should have harmonized in order to live well with themselves. Ditto in the house.

In this discipline, each member of the family corresponds not only to an element of nature, but also a part of the body, an hour of the day, a part of the year, a particular attitude of life. And as Zan the thunder is the first male child corresponding to the east, to the legs, to the impetus of the beginning, so Son is the first female daughter, corresponding to the wind, the belly and the hips, the energy of wood, the moment of beginning also intended as departure, but towards maturation; it is in fact connected to the middle of May, the period in which we all feel better because we wake up from the winter numbness. It is "the gate of man".

Feng Shui is then a way to relate the outside to the inside, the environment to emotions, fathers to children: a way to understand family problems. Looking for problem areas in the house, seeing if there is harmony in them and working on them to modify them is therefore working on our emotions, "on our internal rooms, on our fears". This is the meaning then, "the correlation with our living".

And bioarchitecture? It is connected! If a room does not have colors and materials harmonized with the energy of those who live there (or live with them at this point), it is necessary to paint, add materials, change the order of things. But why natural and eco materials?

FENG SHUI: HOME DESIGN AND COLORS

From my personal experience I have drawn my consequences: a natural and a "normal" painting emanate different sensations. There are different perceptions of them: the plastic wall gives nothing, the others even seem to change their appearance according to the weather, the hours; and with them the sensations change. "They seem to be in motion. And, wow, you can see the difference!"

Natural materials give us more vitality and make us live better. There are, in them, all the elements to rebalance the energies.

In eco-sustainability there is the whole cycle of Yin and Yang - from the earth to the return to it, passing through the other elements and metal - and with it we respect not only the environment, but also people. Plus, there are truly unexpected finishes! Clays with oxides and pigments derived from plants to replace chemical materials, particular fillings instead of resins. Finally, the organic home today is no longer a luxury for a few. Prices are no longer so exorbitant.

Then choosing natural materials is an ethical choice not only to the surrounding world, but also for you.

Integrating Feng Shui and natural materials therefore means introducing into the home something that has life, that produces vibration, that speaks to increase our well-being, understood as vitality, as listening to oneself, as a desire for serenity.

Hence the start of Abitare Consapevole, (Conscious Living) a course dedicated to architects and designers on geobiology - a millenary discipline that studies the interactions of natural energy fields with the biophysical balance of living beings - Feng Shui and bio-architecture, for those who want to pursue a career perhaps closer to the profound meaning of life.

My dream would be to create "talking neighborhoods" and not simple dormitory houses: generally, people do not greet their neighbors! That is, to create houses in which living is a conscious act.

Understanding what is not functional for us. They make things around us safe. The aseptic, on the other hand, is understanding who he is. And will put back objects and colors. Customizing the exterior. Parts of the body, of our life and the rooms. The casino room indicates that you don't know what kind of relationship you want. A background piano accompanies us to the conclusions.

Once again, the things that have been talked about stimulate me and fully suit me. Observe the house to see if it is in balance and act now! Cleaning and eliminating the superfluous, for example, to circulate energy. Observe yourselves and accept yourself.

And change the things that are wrong in the house you are leaving, so as not to find them in the new one: in fact, I have accumulated things for 8 years! And now that I live with only a bed and a sofa because I moved almost 3 months ago and I have thrown practically everything away, so I live better. The "casino room" was my home: I had a mess inside, in a nutshell! And I reflected it, by filling every inch. Casino at home means casino inside. Carelessness of the environment in which we live, carelessness of oneself.

A lot to think about if you want to. Loving oneself always starts from here, from questioning oneself, from wanting to understand one's limits, to overcome them, to see every obstacle as something beyond which one will be better off and not as a cause for depression.

The house is not a wall. So, let's listen to it as if it were a body, as if it were our home body, because the place where we live breathes with us and is reflected in our life.

Working on the house is working on oneself!

FENG SHUI: HOME DESIGN AND COLORS

FENG SHUI: 10 TIPS FOR DECORATING YOUR HOME WITH AWARENESS

Feng Shui is an oriental art, of Chinese origin, which aims to support traditional architecture in the design of homes and in the choice of furniture for furnishing. The spaces are organized in such a way as to create real harmony between the inside and the outside of the house.

The principles of Feng Shui take into account the presence of magnetic and energy fields in the arrangement of furnishings. Each choice is aimed at creating a welcoming environment that can promote the well-being of those who live there. Choosing to furnish your home with awareness, following the principles and advice of Feng Shui, allows you to spend your time in pleasant, comfortable and tidy spaces, suitable for moments of relaxation, to welcome guests, or to work. Feng Shui can in fact also find application in the office. Here are some useful tips for those who are preparing to furnish or renovate their spaces, or simply to tidy up.

1) Decluttering

In Feng Shui, order is the first rule. Before taking care of moving the sofa or the mirror, it is good to get rid of the superfluous. The accumulation of unused or disordered objects, according to Feng Shui, prevents the flow of positive energies and can create situations of stasis that can negatively affect the well-being of home life. It is therefore advisable to try to tidy up every day and get rid of what is not needed, obviously in the most ecological way possible, for example by bartering. Do not accumulate stuff and follow a very simple principle: just enough is the right amount.

2) Colors

If you are going to paint from scratch or repaint the walls of the rooms of the house, pay attention to the colors. The choice must not be random and must be suitable for every environment. In the living room, colors such as red or orange facilitate conversation with family or friends. Blue and green in the bedrooms promote relaxation and restful sleep, while pink stimulates romance and passion. In the kitchen, yellow stimulates the appetite and gives energy from the beginning of the day, starting from the moment of breakfast.

3) Sofa and bed

The arrangement of furniture is one of the key principles of Feng Shui. In the living room, the sofa must be positioned so that it faces the door. Whoever enters the house will immediately perceive the presence of a symbol of welcome and hospitality. It must also be placed with the backrest close to the wall, to give a sense of protection to those who will sit on it. The bed, to create a situation of greater relaxation and tranquility, must be positioned so that it is not directly in front of the door. The door must be out of sight while trying to fall asleep.

4) Mirrors

Mirrors can hinder the flow of positive energies. According to Feng Shui, mirrors should not be placed in the bedroom. Having a mirror near your bed may make it difficult to sleep. A valid suggestion in this regard could consist in placing the mirror on one of the internal doors of the wardrobe or in a corridor outside the room dedicated to the night's rest.

5) Windows

The windows of the house must be large enough to allow optimal use of natural light to illuminate the interior spaces during the day. Particular attention must be paid to windows that are facing a busy street. The passage of cars must not disturb the harmony and tranquility of the house. For this reason, Feng Shui recommends protecting them with suitable light-colored curtains, which do not obstruct the natural light too much.

6) Kitchen

The kitchen must be a welcoming and tidy place. The door should never be positioned so that it is directly behind the cook, in order to promote a feeling of tranquility while at the stove. The stove must always be kept clean, in order to promote abundance and prosperity. The oven should never be placed near the refrigerator or sink. In the kitchen, as in all other rooms, furniture with fluid and rounded shapes should be preferred. Pay particular attention to the edges of the tables.

7) Materials

For home furnishings, Feng Shui suggests the choice of materials that are as natural as possible, such as wood, stone and metal. Therefore, plastic materials should be avoided. The wooden floors and windows allow for continuity, at least from a visual point of view, between the natural external environments and the interior of the house.

8) Bathroom

According to Feng Shui, the bathroom can be placed anywhere in the house. However, there is an important recommendation: the bathroom door should not open directly to the kitchen, in order to prevent the spread of germs. The bathroom should always have a window, in order to allow adequate ventilation and to ensure light conditions that can allow you to use the room without using electricity during the day.

9) Stairs and elevators

The stairs inside the house should always be harmonious and not too steep, as well as formed by steps of regular height and built with natural, resistant materials, such as wood or stone. When designing an office, particular attention should be paid to the position of the stairs or lift relative to the entrance door. As the "Feng Shui Manual " (Wu Xing, Edition II Meeting Point, 2000) suggests, the office should not face an elevator or a steep staircase, as this could hamper financial luck.

10) Garden

The vegetable plot and the garden must always be cared for and in order. Even the plants present inside the house or on the terrace must receive the necessary care to avoid the presence of dry leaves and the perception of a feeling of disorder. The presence of areas of the garden with poorly maintained plants hinders the flow of positive energies, favoring negative emotions. Taking care of the vegetable garden and the garden is in turn a beneficial therapy for the mind and inner well-being.

FENG SHUI: HOME DESIGN AND COLORS

CONSTRUCTIVE PRINCIPLES OF FENG SHUI

In recent times we have witnessed an increasingly widespread diffusion of Feng Shui, the ancient Chinese art of arranging the rooms of a house, an office, a garden, according to very specific energy settings that constitute the foundations of a healthy and harmonious home.

Newspapers, TV, books on the subject, observe this phenomenon closely, publish more and more articles that contain interviews with celebrities but also with ordinary people who live in houses built according to the principles of Feng Shui. For many of them, living in a Feng Shui home means highlighting not only the beauty that it radiates but also the serenity and harmony it infuses.

FENG SHUI: HOME DESIGN AND COLORS

Feeling refreshed in health, affection and work is a characteristic of an environment created on the basis of the principles of Feng Shui.

In reality the question is much more articulated and complex, much more than what is proposed by the books of the sector; to get to master the technique of this art, and get good results, a long and laborious preparation is required through very ancient and complex techniques, but which with the necessary patience and passion can be achieved in a few years.

The Feng Shui phenomenon is still little known and often those who want to know more have to go around the world and directly study the texts written in Chinese or English, since no texts translated into Italian are available, and it is of fundamental importance to have a "direct " and "assiduous" contact with a Master of this art.

The fundamental concept of Feng Shui is nothing short of revolutionary for us: it is based on the principle of a profound "space- time" connection and originates from traditional Chinese medicine which has its roots in the era of the Yellow Emperor, (first emperor of China) who lived well over 2000 years before the birth of Christ; and is considered the founder of Chinese civilization. The Chinese people attribute to him the birth of many traditions of China, including Taoism itself, and the birth of traditional Chinese medicine.

For Feng Shui, a house, a building, an office, a garden, an entire neighborhood has its birth and its "expiration", just like a human being, in the sense that the energies that coexist with it stop functioning at some point, and to restore their correct functioning one always resorts to the art of the Feng Shui Master who, with his intervention, makes these places "come back to life" and allows them to express their function again to the fullest.

FENG SHUI: HOME DESIGN AND COLORS

According to the art of Feng Shui, the place where we live or work, as well as the way of arranging and furnishing spaces, significantly influences the harmonious development of our existence, and a correct arrangement of spaces can develop our creative capacity, facilitate study, stimulate sleep and help us increase our economic resources.

The interior and the exterior, for Eastern philosophy, are interconnected, indissoluble, because the energies that govern the environment are the same ones that control our body. This connection is now forgotten as modern man has moved away from the fundamental forces that govern the universe, for this reason society is divided, restless and separated from the natural world.

When the house 'conforms to the natural principles' there will be harmony and peace.

The vision of the Feng Shui architect is totally holistic, as he faces the problems of the environment for which he is called to intervene, and analyzes the cycles related to time, space and nature.

FENG SHUI: HOME DESIGN AND COLORS

THE FENG SHUI GARDEN. THE ANCIENT CHINESE ART OF MAKING ENERGIES FLOW INTO SPACE

The first steps and the secrets behind creating a Feng Shui garden.

Fire, Earth, Wood, Water and Metal are the 5 building blocks of life on earth. The combination of these elements qualitatively regulates all the mutations of life and nature and are the basis of the creation of a Feng Shui garden.

Feng Shui is a millenary Chinese art that has gone through moments of glory and moments of darkness, that today enjoys new fame and great respect both in the East and in the West, where values and principles have been rediscovered that are applied in the creation of homes but also of important buildings, banks, offices, airports, etc.

But a special role is occupied by the relationship of Feng Shui with greenery and nature, as the cornerstones of the discipline. The Feng Shui garden (from the Chinese Feng "wind" and Shui "water") does not fear the passing of fashions and the confrontation with different landscape cultures, since it has a soft approach, adaptable to any place and climate, and its goal is offering an oasis of beauty, peace and sustainability.

At the basis of Feng Shui are the concepts of Chi, Yin and Yang and the Five Elements, from which all the possible combinations between nature and architecture develop. The Chi is the Vital Energy and represents the force of energy that generates, transports and destroys life, in a continuous, cyclical motion; its correct movement and distribution allow us and all of nature to live.

From the principle of the Tao derive the two complementary and opposite forces of Yin and Yang; when these forces work in harmony, they do not generate conflict, but are interdependent, as one generates the other in a continuous movement. The interaction of these forces with the 5 Elements and their continuous and tireless cycle generates everything that surrounds us and ourselves, creating always different and unique combinations.

FENG SHUI: HOME DESIGN AND COLORS

The culture of Feng Shui has great respect for nature and its manifestations. Nothing is underestimated, no animate or inanimate form is damaged, no natural element is moved or eliminated if it is not strictly necessary, even the grass is cut very little, and plants and flowers are cut only in exceptional cases, not as a typical custom. Respect for the lifeblood that circulates in plant forms is considered on a par with the blood that circulates in our veins, and the healing and regenerating powers of plants have been transmitted by the Chinese for millennia.

Of nature, Feng Shui does not consider only the plant forms, but the whole, as in a large throbbing organism: water, minerals, rocks, stones and sand, etc. Natural phenomena are considered with the same attention: rain, wind, snow, drought, etc., and their impact on a territory, therefore they are always observed before building a green space or a house. Feng Shui is also expressed by symbols; it is there that we can understand the language of nature and that we can introduce elements that represent a missing or weak natural force.

In order for a stay in a Feng Shui garden to be pleasant, it is necessary to intervene on a series of basic factors, which in a simple way favor the circulation of energy.

First of all, it must be a varied and luxuriant environment, which alternates deciduous and evergreen plants, preferring species of local origin.

Without exaggerating in quantity, we check the health of the plants already present. We introduce new species, one at a time, considering the type of foliage and the color of flowers or fruits, leaving the necessary space for them to develop easily, and providing for the juxtaposition with the pre-existing ones. We try to favor plants with rounded, soft or tall and slender shapes, avoiding those with thorns or sharp leaves, which create a negative energy (Sha). Tall hedges and bushes can be useful for creating a protective barrier, but let's avoid creating an overwhelming wall that isolates the inside of the garden too much from the outside.

If we have to create a garden for a house, we create access to it with a sinuous path, avoiding a straight line that points directly to the door, or if this is not possible, we interrupt the path by placing a fountain, a flower bed or a bench in the middle. Drinking fountains, troughs and feeders attract small animals and help to liven up and increase the Chi; flowers and aromatic plants will do the same thing.

In any case, it is important to have an overview of the area and of what already exists; we decide whether to include a naturalistic or architectural detail in our view, creating the space between the trees to see it and highlight it, and if we want to exclude a bad view, we can do it by creating hedges or trellises with vines.

The great variety of plants that can be used cannot be summarized in a few lines, but what interests us is to try to develop a sensitivity that allows us to identify, even by ourselves, which are the best activators of Chi for our garden. It is important to use the species present in our areas, which contain an energetic strength and a particular symbolism. Flowering plants are excellent activators of Chi since they combine the strength of the green with the colors and perfumes of the inflorescences; Feng Shui prefers flowering plants to cut flowers and it is important in the choice to imagine the combination after flowering, considering not only the colors, but also the shape of the leaves and the size it can reach.

Trees for Feng Shui are the quintessence of nature itself. Their presence creates the reference point in a green space, generates a micro-system, balances vital functions, absorbs pollutants and protects the homes. For this reason, we feel more relaxed in their presence.

Finally, a Feng Shui garden does not love symmetry too much, since the energy to circulate easily requires sinuous, soft, free shapes, so it is better to avoid corners, edges, straight and aggressive lines. We always try to balance empty and full spaces, colorful and evergreen plants, smooth and rough surfaces, stones, rocks and water, in a harmonious, varied, but not too redundant and suffocating whole. We always leave room for a new arrival, a flower sprouted from seeds carried by the wind, a nest among dry branches, a plant received as a gift. Let the energy flow, let nature take its course and enjoy all its beauty.

Feng shui is an ancient Chinese science whose rules outline how to build and order in the best way the environments in which you live. The principles underlying feng shui are based on the harmonious relationship between man and nature; since every man is constantly conditioned by the influences coming

FENG SHUI: HOME DESIGN AND COLORS

from the outside, it is preferable to choose to live every day in an environment that is full of positive energies.

According to feng shui thinking, the conformation of the spaces in which we work, study or live is really able to influence our inner well-being, our happiness and even our wealth. So, let's see some practical tips to transform the furnishings of our homes and to improve our inner health thanks to it.

Entrance and garden

The entrance area is a very important part of the house. It must make guests perceive a feeling of welcome and should therefore respect the following parameters. The door should first of all be able to open inwards so as not to force those who arrive to move back. The very first room you enter should be well lit, clean, tidy and with pale colored walls.

Furniture should be sparse and coats should be stored in a closet to allow energy to flow freely into the home. Also for this reason it is important that the furniture and other elements such as roofs and doormats are free of edges. Mirrors and paintings, on the other hand, are very useful as they increase the perception of openness and size.

Even the paths leading to the entrance should suggest an idea of hospitality and it is for this reason that we tend to advise against the angled, broken lines and the presence of flowers that hinder the passage. The garden path should therefore follow a curved path and be free from any bulky plants or shrubs. Trees and climbing plants can be placed near the house as long as they do not cover the view of doors and windows with their leaves.

To have an energetically balanced garden it is necessary to correctly balance the yin and yang elements. Both the garden and the balcony are in fact natural extensions of the house and must be organized with the same attention and care reserved for the interior spaces. The plants and flowers chosen for the outdoors should be of many different varieties and should be arranged in an off-center position.

FENG SHUI: HOME DESIGN AND COLORS

Feng Shui Garden and Driveway

Feng shui conceives plants as true symbols; before choosing them, it is therefore necessary to know their meanings. For example, the evergreens represent stability and longevity while the deciduous trees symbolize change: to have a harmonious garden it is therefore necessary to have both.

Also, for the principle of balancing yin and yang, it is essential that the garden is equipped in the same way with areas of light and areas of shadow. Since the literal meaning of the feng shui expression is "wind and water", objects that recall these two elements cannot be missing in the garden. Fountains, small ponds, flags, pinwheels, wind games and other moving objects serve to make the garden more aesthetically beautiful but also to better circulate the energies present in it.

Finally, other aspects not to be underestimated are sound, smell and touch; these factors also contribute to improving the mood and making the home undoubtedly a more comfortable place. It is therefore advisable to enrich the balcony and / or the garden with aromatic herbs, stones, Tibetan bells and everything that can help instill pleasant sensations in the body.

BRING BALANCE AND HARMONY TO THE HOME WITH THE ART OF FENG SHUI, PLACING THE EMPHASIS ON THE ENVIRONMENT AROUND US AND ON WELL-BEING

Western culture has difficulty in thinking that the arrangement of furniture inside the house can have a beneficial effect on the harmony of life of those who live there. The Chinese Feng Shui philosophy argues that it is very important to furnish the house following real rules that will help to convey positive energies inside the houses. Let's see three rules together to bring a positive energy flow with Feng Shui into the home, just in time for the new year 2021.

FENG SHUI: HOME DESIGN AND COLORS

1. Clean up the house for balance and good energy flow

Feng Shui is an ancient Chinese practice that helps to align the external environment with inner well-being and emotional needs. By inviting a good flow of energy into the home, good health, luck and wealth will follow. The first step in starting this process is decluttering as much as possible. For those who do not know what this term means, decluttering is not the simple elimination of superfluous objects, it is a real attitude oriented towards the essential. A liberation that opens up the future and new possibilities.

Tidying up is a great way to start the new year with a clean slate. For those who know me and follow me on social media, they know of my Persian origin. In fact, in Iran the Persian New Year is celebrated every year with the arrival of spring and one of the rites for the New Year is cleaning the house. A very ancient custom close to Feng Shui. A clean home works wonders for our mental clarity and overall health. In feng shui, each space is connected to the other, and allows positive energy to flow throughout the house. My advice is to add a decorative mirror to the living room to make the space seem larger and multiply the flow of positive energy. Meanwhile, cupboards or drawers overloaded with old items block chi (energy), so it's best to discard all clutter.

2. Create a relaxing space

Incorporate the Yin (feminine) and Yang (masculine) concept into the decor. Ying and Yang are two conflicting forces that cannot exist without each other. By mixing different forms together, this concept can be applied. Are you wondering how? Here's an example: Contrast the sharp edges of the carpets with the soft curves of a sofa or mirror in the living room. Thus, there will be balance in the room and a more relaxing atmosphere is created.

Creating a relaxing and peaceful environment in the bedroom is very important, because it is the resting place. To maintain a relaxing atmosphere, mirrors must be removed or hidden to avoid an energy overload in the space. While for furniture placement, the bed must be the main focus of the room. Place it on the side opposite the door, against a wall and sleep with your head facing north. In fact, it would seem that the magnetic north pole of the earth, which corresponds to the positive pole of the human body, has a favorable influence and increases the duration of sleep.

3. Productivity in the Home Office

Due to the coronavirus crisis, many companies have found themselves catapulted into home working. And the crisis is not over yet, which is why many employees still work from home, fully or partially. For which it is necessary to dedicate a well-designed space for the home office. As this room places an emphasis on productivity, the desk should be the main focus here. It is also important to use the right accessories to keep a tidy space. Use plants to invite positive energy and cool the home. In feng shui, they are commonly associated as a life force and bring growth, prosperity and luck. The plants I recommend to use in the office are the money plant, the lucky bamboo and the peace lily.

FENG SHUI: HOME DESIGN AND COLORS

TIDY UP YOUR HOME TO ATTRACT WEALTH, LOVE, HEALTH

By putting these simple tips into practice, you can greatly improve the quality of your life. According to the ancient practice of Feng Shui, the house is an organism that breathes and its breath is the vital energy that flows in the corridors and in the rooms, entering and exiting through doors and windows.

When its flow passes undisturbed it transmits serenity and tranquility. Feng Shui literally means "wind and water" because like the man who hoists the sail to move the boat or who dips the mill wheel in the river to make it work, when we want something, we make nature do it for us. Feng Shui helps to bring together this energy that surrounds us positively and harmoniously to our advantage.

The Bagua (represented on the left in the image) is a map necessary to identify the areas of the house with respect to the energy forces. You can represent on paper the plan of your house, one sheet for each floor.

Place the bagua so that the career side is at the entrance to the house and thus the zones and their relationship with the energy forces will be clear (represented on the right in the image). In this way we can identify the various areas of our life that need improvement or where we want to strengthen positive energy by intervening with Feng Shui remedies.

We can also use the Bagua inside each room, superimposing it on the plan of each single room, thus carrying out an in-depth investigation. In fact, the method applies both to the entire house and to each single room.

The wall where your entrance door to the apartment is located (and the door of each room for when you go to analyze them individually) must always correspond to the side of the diagram on which you find the 3 points of: KNOWLEDGE (left corner) - CAREER - FRIENDS (right corner).

FENG SHUI: HOME DESIGN AND COLORS

The eight elements of the Bagua corresponding to the eight zones of the house are: career, knowledge, family, money, reputation (fame), marriage, children, friends (communication, travel, useful people).

DISORDER AND DIRT ARE SYMPTOMS OF NEGATIVE ENERGY

Now look at which points of the house there are furniture or clusters of objects that create an obstruction and now look at which area of the diagram they are positioned to understand which area of your life is temporarily obstructed.

Just as if we find confusion in the children's area it means concern about them or their creative projects.

It is also recommended to remove objects and drawers from under the bed as they prevent our energy from flowing and re-charging.

In fact, in addition to manifesting itself unconsciously as a psychological reaction to a problem present in a specific sector of our life, it can also become the cause of this problem. The disordered accumulations would thus represent a real obstacle to the vital flow stopping that existential area developing positively.

Throw away all the old things you don't use. The old things you keep in the house, which are superfluous and useless, tend to absorb negative energies. And they make you feel bad, making the past return to the present, when instead you have to think about the future. If you want to give a blow to the past, close the door in its face, throw away everything you don't need, keep only the things you use. You will benefit a lot in the future.

The house must always be clean and tidy and without accumulation of dirt; we eliminate rugs, canvases, doilies, unnecessary fabrics from the rooms. They tend to accumulate dirt, and make breathing difficult. We need to make the positive energy flow well into the house.

FENG SHUI: HOME DESIGN AND COLORS

LET'S CLEAN, TIDY, AND USE THE RIGHT REMEDIES

After analyzing and removing the messy spots in your home, it is possible to enhance those areas with new objects related to that specific area.

Many negative life events can be avoided or mitigated by simply following a few simple guidelines. The arrangement of the furniture, the direction in which the head of the bed is placed, the colors and the ornaments present contribute to create a relaxing and stimulating environment for people.

The remedies can be fountains, wind chimes, plants and flowers, mirrors, lights, and objects that represent what corresponds to the topic, for example an angel to reinforce the aid area, which will be placed in the area where you intend to balance or strengthen the energy.

UPGRADE CAREER: blue or black objects, paintings depicting seascapes, wind bells on the front door, an exciting image or statuette that can be a stimulus for you, a model to follow, an energy generator.

ENHANCE WEALTH: blue, purple or red objects, bowl full of coins, a crassula plant with a gold coin in the soil, even a purple (color of prosperity) casket perhaps with gold designs, a fountain with moving water.

ENHANCE HEALTH: strengthened by everything that represents growth, therefore the green color, plants, flowers and wooden objects.

ENHANCE LOVE: pink, red or white objects; always put them in pairs like two hearts, two flowers, two teddy bears in order to favor romantic relationships.

POWER CREATIVITY: objects in pastel and white colors, made of metal, such as paintings, tables, lamps, chandeliers, everything related to creativity and children, therefore paper and pencils, stereos, musical instruments.

ENHANCE FAME: red color, give a lot of light to this area ("let's put ourselves in prominence"), triangular shapes, awards and everything that connects us to fame and notoriety.

FENG SHUI: HOME DESIGN AND COLORS

ENHANCE FRIENDS: objects of gray, white or black color or anything that symbolizes metal, crystals.

BOOST KNOWLEDGE: black, blue and green colors, books, study area.

In the East, where there is a more advanced culture of housing than ours, everything is always kept in order and in harmony. We follow the advice of this ancient people who have a deep knowledge of energies and the world.

FENG SHUI: HOME DESIGN AND COLORS

BAGUA METHOD TO ATTRACT LUCK IN THE DIFFERENT SECTORS OF THE HOUSE

With this method you will only get tangible results in rooms you use regularly. It is important that all the rooms in the house are well ventilated and can benefit from the energy that comes from the light of the sun.

To identify the area of the house corresponding to the type of luck you want to activate, you can divide the space according to the pie chart. Overlay the circular scheme of the compass on the plan of the environment under consideration and then divide the space into sectors, from the central point towards the outside according to the lines of emanation of the Chi. Each sector thus takes the form of a slice of cake.

At this point, decide according to your judgment which rooms to activate based on where you spend the most time.

For maximum results, give space to your creativity and your personal taste. Do not exhibit paintings that do not meet your taste. Listen to your inner voice.

To create a happy living environment, think about what gives you energy and try to convey it in terms of decoration, furniture and furnishing accessories.

- THE SOUTH BRINGS ACKNOWLEDGMENT - The south is associated with the LI trigram, which means the fire of light, Yang energy and success. The south is also associated with the horse, the phoenix and the snake, 3 auspicious symbols that mean fame and recognition. By activating the warm southern energy in the right place in the house through one or more of these symbols or through the color red, luck is stimulated for success: fame, recognition of one's talents and popularity.

- THE NORTH BRINGS LUCK TO THE CAREER - the north is associated with the trigram KAN, which means water. By activating the northern sector of the house with water you will see rapid results in career and business. An aquarium located in the north, for example, is an effective tool as a luck activator. However, you can also use small objects containing water or inspired by the

FENG SHUI: HOME DESIGN AND COLORS

theme of water, such as a painting. It also has a beneficial effect to paint the north wall blue, or to paint it white, silver or gold as, according to the production cycle of the elements, the metal activates the water. For the same reason, you can arrange the stereo system to the north, which has many metallic elements. Instead, do not activate water in the bedroom as it can cause leaks.

- EAST BRINGS GOOD HEALTH - east is associated with the trigram CHEN, which means wood. For feng shui, the east is a very important direction because it is the home of the Green Dragon, one of the 4 celestial animals of the Chinese zodiac and the symbol of auspicious luck. East is the best part of the house to place dragons. Arranging the image of the dragon on the eastern part of the living room, the dragon must hold a symbolic pearl and spit water. A single celestial creature or a maximum of 5 is sufficient, but not for those born in the year of the dragon (1928, 1940, 1952, 1964, 1976, 1988, 2000, 2012) or those who occupy a high position in government and business. Placing the dragon figure in or near the water. By activating the east one obtains health, longevity and luck in the offspring. To activate it you can use decorative wooden objects or plants. You can also choose a tree made of semi-precious stones such as citrine or aventurine (do not use synthetic crystals) with a solid trunk to ensure a stable base, or decorated with symbolic coins and a red or gold ribbon.

- THE WEST ACTIVATES THE FAMILY LUCK - the west is associated with the trigram of joy, TUI, which is also called the trigram of the lake or the river and the White Tiger, one of the 4 celestial animals of the Chinese zodiac. If the Chi of the west side of the house is protected and energized, the family is united and remains healthy and strong and all its members will enjoy a long life. West belongs to the metal element and its color is white. There is no need to expose the white tiger indoors, just activate the metal element. The best activators are gold coins from China and Taiwan, but also other gold objects.

- SOUTHWEST BRINGS LOVE - Southwest is the home of KUN, the matriarchal trigram that increases luck in love and the beginning of a new phase of life for those in the age of marriage. Place in the southwest the symbol of double happiness or various propitiatory symbols such as red peonies, mandarin ducks, crystal balls ... the best way to activate the southwest is to avoid that this place of the house is occupied by the presence of a bathroom, a closet or the kitchen.

FENG SHUI: HOME DESIGN AND COLORS

- THE NORTHWEST GUARANTEES PROTECTION - the northwest is associated with the CHIEN trigram, the trigram of the sky that symbolizes good fortune linked to powerful benefactors. If you wish to receive support from your boss, this is the sector of the house to activate. Its element is metal and in Chinese culture metal also means gold. If you keep a vase full of coins in the northwest corner of the house or bury a symbolic chest in the northwest corner of the garden, it will benefit the patriarch of the family.

- THE SOUTHEAST BRINGS PROSPERITY - the southeast is associated with the SUN trigram, whose element is wood. If you want to have more income, you need to energize the southeast corner with plants and flowers. When the flowers wither, replace them with others. Remember to always eliminate dead plants.

- THE NORTHEAST BRINGS LUCK TO STUDIES - the north-east is associated with the trigram of the mountain, which alludes to the effort of preparation and training to reach the summit. The most useful symbol for this purpose is the crystal ball. You can also use a crystal paperweight. You can also buy a natural single-pointed crystal and have it become his amulet for your child during his studies.

FENG SHUI: HOME DESIGN AND COLORS

FENG SHUI: THE PRINCIPLES AND RULES OF THE ANCIENT CHINESE DISCIPLINE

This ancient discipline is a set of decoding practices of the environment, landscape and interior spaces of buildings with the aim of avoiding the onset of negative energies that over time can affect man and his daily life.

This ancient doctrine has Chinese and Tibetan origins while in Japan the equivalent is called Ka-so. Still very present in the East, in fact, when you buy a house or land, a Feng Shui master is first consulted.

The harmony of the universe depends on the balance between two principles: The Yin, the female sex and the moon and the Yang, the male sex and the sun.

Here, together with the concept of beauty, considerable importance is given to the subtle balances and energies of a place.

This art, in the design of homes, combines traditional architecture with a search for balance and harmony between the inside and the outside. Feng Shui, even in the arrangement of furniture, considers magnetic and energy fields. Nothing is chosen at random but everything is positioned with a rule that aims at the well-being of those who live in the environment.

We put awareness into what we do!

Some general rules of Feng Shui

Before moving on to home and office furnishings, here are some general rules if you want to adopt the doctrine of Feng Shui too.

The Chi energies that are found in the environment must interact positively with the person, stimulate him and make him feel calm. The walls that surround us must give us positivity, the environment must increase our self-esteem and make us feel good.

FENG SHUI: HOME DESIGN AND COLORS

Make order - declutter. You have to get rid of the superfluous, you have to throw out unnecessary things and tidy up. According to this doctrine only in this way can you allow a flow of positive energies. After a healthy cleaning, you just need to stop accumulating things in the future that you know will not be of any use to you.

The colors that decorate a house are also very important to foster positive energies. Choose blue and green for the rooms to promote relaxation or pink to let passion flow. For the living room, on the other hand, choose orange or red, colors suitable for facilitating sharing. Finally, color the kitchen yellow to stimulate appetite and energy!

Water, an element linked to money and communication, must always be present in the rooms of the house and it is important to have a quiet river or lake near the house.

Furnish your home and office according to the principles of Feng Shui

The space that we live in every day is decorated according to certain rules because right here you are creating the energies and vibrations that are positive to make is that our personalities are well and in balance with the house.

Bedroom: must be located away from the street and the front door. The bed should be placed transversely, with the head facing east, in the corner diagonally opposite the head and feet should not point towards the room entrance. Do not place mirrors in the bedroom, they have the ability to disturb the energy field. During the night, cover them with a towel and you will see the quality of sleep will tend to improve considerably.

Eliminate from the room elements such as the PC and the mobile phone, which steal energy.

Living room: in this room the sofa must be placed facing the entrance door to emphasize the welcome towards the guest, and against a wall to emphasize a sense of protection.

Kitchen: here too positive energies must circulate, respecting the cardinal points, and negative ones must disappear. How is it prepared? How do you

FENG SHUI: HOME DESIGN AND COLORS

cook? Which dishes to use? Also, for these topics there is a precise rule according to Feng Shui. The place must always be tidy and clean and the door should not stand behind the cook, in order to promote tranquility. The oven should stay away from both the refrigerator and the sink, and the shapes of the furniture should be soft and without edges. There must also be harmony in food. To better digest legumes, use chilli!

Bathroom: This can be anywhere in the house. The important thing is that the bathroom door does not overlook the kitchen, in order to prevent the spread of germs, and that this has a window to ventilate.

Garden: cared for in every detail with plants arranged and without dry leaves. An unloved garden attracts negative energies. Having a green thumb also helps your inner balance.

Office: The desk should be placed so that your gaze is directed towards the window or door and your back is protected. Do not place it facing the wall but prefer an open view in order to increase and develop your Chi. The office should not be facing an elevator or a steep staircase. This could prevent the energy from staying in the room.

This oriental practice has important repercussions on everyday life. Try to furnish your home according to the principles of Feng Shui to improve the flow of positive energy and feel better.

Besides the beauty of your house do they that energy forces are not locked into it from a poorly placed furniture. Think that even a door that opens badly can negatively affect the energy!

Day after day we can also apply these small but effective Feng Shui tricks to our home, don't you think?

FENG SHUI: HOME DESIGN AND COLORS

10 THINGS NOT TO HAVE AT HOME ACCORDING TO FENG SHUI

About to furnish your home or give it a breath of fresh air? Here are 10 things to eliminate or modify immediately according to Feng Shui to regain energy and harmony.

We all would like a long life, full of love and the possibility of exploiting energies and great opportunities and according to Feng Shui, at least at home, a few small tricks would be enough to create excellent conditions for harmony and success.

According to this oriental discipline which has as its main objective the right balance with the environment, any piece of furniture or object is able to condition our inner energy, especially in the place where we should feel most comfortable and at ease.

However, there are many mistakes that we make every day that break that chain of energy and ruin the atmosphere: whether it is an object that has not been repaired for a long time, a dry plant or the bed not arranged properly, the list of things to avoid at home according to Feng Shui is definitely long.

Here are the 10 most common wrong situations that interfere with the harmony of your home.

Did you just realize you were wrong? Don't panic - the solution is just a click away!

1. Different floors in the same room

Metaphor of the strength of the house, according to Feng Shui, it is preferable to choose only one floor for the whole apartment or at least for each room. In this way the attracted energy will be continuous and homogeneous.

2. Mirrors in the bedroom

FENG SHUI: HOME DESIGN AND COLORS

Abolishing the mirrors in the bedroom would be ideal to avoid receiving reflected energy during sleep and thus always feeling tired, but we recognize that it would be a little exaggerated. In this case, Feng Shui offers us a compromise, suggesting us not to place them against the door, in front of the windows or the bed and in any case never arranged on two opposite walls, thus avoiding creating a vortex of energy that bounces aggressively.

3. Furniture and objects with edges

The flow of energies should always be continuous and positive in all rooms of the house. Among the things to avoid for Feng Shui the use of furniture and objects with extremely square edges and shapes, which break a harmonious balance ensured by rounded decorations and sinuous shapes.

4. Beds, sofas or desks with their back to the door

Maybe you also feel it subconsciously and it is certainly linked to our survival instinct, but nobody likes not knowing or not being able to see what is happening behind us. Better then to change the arrangement of the furniture by moving sofas, beds and desks in front of the door. If this is not possible, help yourself with mirrors so that you can see when someone enters or leaves a room.

5. TV in the bedroom

It is said that this kills sociability and more specifically the passion in the bedroom, but the TV is also an electronic device that is not really healthy for our psychophysical well-being. Avoid sleeping with the device on or, better yet, having one in the bedroom. It could give a positive change to your sleep and, why not, rekindle the flame under the covers.

6. Sad or disturbing photographs and images

They could also be beautiful, intense and impactful, but the images and paintings depicting sad and fearful situations or faces should be totally eliminated from the house inspired by the principles of Feng Shui because they negatively affect the atmosphere and mood of those who live there. Better to prefer photographs and images that are lively, relaxing and in any case in perfect harmony, even chromatically, with the environment in which you live.

7. Black bed linen

Undoubtedly trendy, black blankets and sheets are unfortunately banned from Feng Shui because they would negatively affect the energy of the room. Who really does not want to give it up, could soften the dark tones with white pillows or accessories of lighter and more lively shades in contrast with the bed?

8. Broken things

If an object doesn't work why not repair it or get rid of it completely? Having broken objects in the house affects the harmonious flow of energy and is a symptom of carelessness that is also reflected in the person. Better not procrastinate, and act immediately!

9. Bed against the wall

According to Feng Shui, energy should circulate around the bed, especially during sleep. Having a side of the bed in a corner or against a wall would not allow the regeneration of this energy, without considering that, in an emergency or danger condition (don't want to ...) it would be a big obstacle and as a couple it would put you or the your partner at a disadvantage.

10. Dead plants in the house or on the balcony

Isn't your thumb absolutely green? Better to buy succulents or not have any if the alternative is to reduce them at the end of their life and let them dry out. Living in a green environment is certainly essential for our well-being, but by green we also mean beautiful to look at, healthy and thriving: after all, the message to be transmitted is that only life enters your home, right?

FENG SHUI: HOME DESIGN AND COLORS

WHAT ARE THE GOOD (AND BAD) PLANTS FOR FENG SHUI?

In addition to enhancing the aesthetics of a space, plants bring the energy of nature into the home or office. And according to the principles of Feng Shui, houseplants can nourish and heal personal energy, as well as move it from room to room. But when it comes to identifying the best plants for good energy in the home, for Feng Shui there are some guidelines to follow.

Plants and Feng Shui

Decorating the apartment with live plants reinforces the energy of a particular Feng Shui element: wood. The wood element brings vital energy of growth and action to living spaces. It can also inspire compassion, kindness, and resilience. In addition, the green color of plants is associated with healing.

There are not necessarily good and bad Feng Shui plants. After all, the key to Feng Shui is to see the interconnectedness of duality. That said, there are plants that are more commonly recommended for Feng Shui, and plants that can be difficult to maintain good energy in the home.

The best Feng Shui plants

In general, most plants are great for Feng Shui as long as you take good care of them. Plants with soft, rounded leaves are typically best, as they attract and give off a gentle, nourishing energy.

Here are some of them:

Palma Areca (Palm of Bethel)

This is an excellent plant for purifying the air and for Feng Shui. The Areca palm can outgrow many other houseplants and has beautiful fan-shaped leaves. It needs intense, indirect light.

Boston fern or Nephrolepis

Boston ferns are easy to care for indoors as long as you have enough light. The petite versions are perfect for small spaces and for hanging. According to Feng

Shui, all hanging objects help to circulate good energy better and to have more vitality.

Mother-in-law's tongue

Also known as the snake plant, mother-in-law's tongue is a great plant for beginners. It has excellent protective energy qualities for Feng Shui, although it is pointed with long leaves.

Jade

Also called the money plant, this succulent features many rounded leaves. This gives it a soft and lush look.

Lucky bamboo

Bamboo represents growth and adaptability to change, flexible yet resilient. In the use of Feng Shui, the number of stems has a symbolic meaning. For example, two stems should nourish the areas of life associated with love and three stems nourish happiness. Suitable for bedrooms.

Golden Pothos (Potos)

The golden Pothos is easy to care for and propagate. It grows luxuriantly, its heart-shaped leaves develop along twining branches that climb up any support. It has excellent qualities as an "air purifier".

Like the Boston fern, the Potos can also be hung and this solution propagates its aerial energy.

Challenging plants of Feng Shui

In Feng Shui, there is a concept, the sha Chi, or acute or destructive energy. Sharp objects attack positive energy. Spiky and thorny plants such as cacti are also to be avoided because they disrupt the circulation of energy in the house. Placing them in living areas increases the risk of quarrels and arguments, while in sleeping areas they can make people rest badly. Also, neglected and poorly

FENG SHUI: HOME DESIGN AND COLORS

maintained plants can block energy, so before bringing them indoors, make sure you have the right time and environment to keep them healthy.

FENG SHUI AND PLANTS IN THE HOUSE: THE IDEAL LOCATIONS

As for the choice of plants to use in this environment, we recommend aromatic herbs, especially rosemary, which can make the environment more positive.

But what is the relationship between plants and Feng Shui? According to this oriental philosophy, arranging the plants correctly within the domestic environment, would have the ability to positively influence our mood. Here are some tips on how to best place your plants indoors to benefit from their powerful energies.

ENTRANCE

The entrance is particularly important in Feng Shui, as it is in this environment that the Chi energy from the universe is encountered. The main elements to take into consideration are order and cleanliness, so as to convey a positive impression to your guests. For this reason, it is suggested to furnish this area with a plant capable of attracting attention: the spathiphyllum is among the species most recommended by Feng Shui, being a typical plant of the Amazon rainforest, it does not require a lot of light, produces beautiful white flowers and can be a good furnishing solution.

LIVING ROOM

The most vital area of the house, a space destined not only to welcome guests, but also to experience moments of personal relaxation. For the living room, Feng Shui recommends plants such as cacti or tillandsia (aerial plant that does not grow in pots but suspended). Arranged on the right side of TV or PC screens, these plants will help attenuate the radiation from these electronic devices.

FENG SHUI: HOME DESIGN AND COLORS

KITCHEN

Plants and feng shui are in close contact when it comes to this environment. The kitchen, in fact, is one of the most important areas according to oriental philosophy; this is not surprising when you think about the incredible power of food on our physical and mental state. As for the choice of plants to use in this environment, we recommend aromatic herbs, especially rosemary, which can make the environment more positive.

BEDROOM

This is also a particularly important environment: improving one's sleep quality, thanks to a well-harmonized and balanced place, can significantly affect our well-being. For this environment, Feng Shui recommends keeping a mint plant in the bedroom capable of perfuming the environment with its fresh fragrance, but also (so it seems!) to calm the mind, thus limiting discussion. Among other things, with the right amount of light, this plant will be able to produce essential oils, ideal for fighting stress, fatigue and insomnia.

But plants and Feng Shui don't always get along. In fact, healthy and well cared for plants are able to increase the circulation of Chi in the environment, on the contrary dry leaves and unhealthy plants will cause the opposite effect. If you intend to furnish your home according to the principles of Feng Shui, be careful: treat your plants with care and a lot of love!

FENG SHUI: HOME DESIGN AND COLORS

FURNISH SMALL HOUSES WITH FENG SHUI

The house furnished according to Feng Shui, room by room

Feng Shui can give many ideas to those interested in creating balanced decor and bringing a harmonious atmosphere into the home.

This ancient Taoist art, which has come back into vogue after a few years of silence, takes into account colors and furniture arrangements to make the home healthier and more comfortable, often giving very pleasant results.

It is not necessary to be an orientalist fanatic or a follower of some New Age vein to put into practice at least some of the salient points of Feng Shui, always bearing in mind that this discipline is not absolute and that there are several valid but discordant schools of thought.

There are no mandatory choices, but you have to learn with practice following your instinct and listen to what you need for your well-being.

Let's go from room to room to understand what you can really do to make your home a better place:

Entrance

Balance starts from the entrance. The entrance door must always be well maintained, clean and attractive in appearance. Color is also important: according to Feng Shui, if the door faces north, it should have cold tones, warm south, east green and west white or very light.

It is preferable to avoid placing mirrors, bathrooms or corner walls in front of the front door.

In the case of very small entrances, it is not advisable to have a staircase directly in front of the main entrance door, but if it is a large enough entrance, it is not a problem.

According to some, the house number can also have its importance, since some numbers are considered positive, others negative, but we would go into the field of numerology and... this is not the right place!

Living area

The salon must always be well organized and clean, to encourage conversation between guests and if possible be divided into two distinct areas, but in harmony with each other.

The windows must always be clean and free from clutter, so as to allow the entry of natural light but at the same time protect privacy once the evening has arrived.

If there is a fireplace, it is not advisable to place an aquarium nearby: Feng Shui gives great importance to natural elements and Fire and Water could come into conflict.

Kitchen

Aromatic herbs should never be lacking in the kitchen to add freshness and vibrant energy connected to nature. According to Feng Shui, it is not advisable to have the kitchen too close to the front door to avoid the escape of positive energies.

The kitchen should also have different lighting levels and be spacious, clean, bright and welcoming. Considering the importance of natural light, a large window, perhaps close to the sink, cannot be missing.

Although in the kitchen you need several tools, it is good to avoid the accumulation of unnecessary objects and also to keep this space of the house organized and free from the superfluous.

Bedroom

First of all, it would be much better to avoid computers, TVs and exercise equipment in this room. The bedroom must be a relaxing, peaceful and quiet space, free from distractions.

FENG SHUI: HOME DESIGN AND COLORS

Windows should be opened often and, if possible, an air purifier is recommended to keep the air fresh and oxygen-rich at all times.

In addition to the TV, mirrors are also not approved of, because they upset the harmony of the room, especially in front of the bed. Even in European traditions, mirrors are often frowned upon in the bedroom: it is better to insert a full-length mirror inside a wardrobe door and indulge in mirrors of desired shapes and sizes in other areas of the house.

The bed is obviously very important: in addition to being of the right height and of good quality, it should be positioned as far as possible from the door and have a supporting wall behind the headboard.

Bathroom

Getting a harmonious bathroom is not easy: first of all it should not be in the center of the house, as it is considered negative by Feng Shui. The bathroom should be a real home wellness center in which to take a break and relax, away from everyday stresses.

In this case, mirrors are welcome and indeed double the positive aspects of the Water element. Here, too, different sources of lighting are welcome, even artificial ones (candles included). In this case, functionality and philosophy go hand in hand!

Children's room

It is not easy to apply the principles of Feng Shui in the nursery, but we can take some useful tips in this case too. Fresh and clean air is obviously the first must, Feng Shui or not!

Children love vibrant colors, but it is necessary to choose harmonious shades that do not lead to overexcitation of the little ones, who are significantly more subject to the effects of colors.

Even the children's room should always be clean and tidy, which is achieved over time by patiently teaching your children how to organize toys, giving them the possibility of being able to do it easily thanks to containers and bins.

FENG SHUI: HOME DESIGN AND COLORS

To personalize the room, children's drawings will be enough, usually stimulating and creative, lively and unique. Do not forget for the photo walls related to beautiful and pleasant moments.

Nursery

In this case it is necessary to create a calm, peaceful and harmonious environment, free from clutter and chaos, without annoying or too bright colors. It is good to keep the room organized and free of unnecessary objects. The crib, as in the case of an adult bedroom, should not be too close or aligned with the door. For the colors, all light and pastel shades are welcome, but it is better to try something different from the usual pink and blue. Here, too, the lights should be adaptable to different hours of the day and of different intensity to create a pleasant environment.

Dining room

A round or oval table is considered better than a square or rectangular table, because it brings people together and allows for greater interaction.

The chairs should match the table and give solid back support. The plates should be round, but even square ones are not badly viewed by Feng Shui, they just have a slower energy and are closer to the Earth element.

The choice of colors in this case is very personal, but if you want to listen to the advice of chromotherapy, blue is a color that suppresses the appetite, while warm colors like red, orange and yellow stimulate it.

Home office / study

First of all, it is important that the home office is as far away from the bedroom as possible. Let yourself go and follow your creativity, because this space must reflect the personality of those who occupy it.

Air quality and natural light are also crucial here and large and spacious windows should be present if possible.

The desk should not face the door and be as far away from it as possible, or away from its line. Also in this case, disorder is prohibited, because it affects productivity and the ability to concentrate ...

FENG SHUI: HOME DESIGN AND COLORS

THE FIVE ELEMENTS IN FENG SHUI

In Feng Shui everything that moves around us is Energy, manifesting itself through the vibrations of the Five Elements. The balance of the five elements in the home and work spaces are the basis of our well-being.

THE CYCLES OF THE FIVE ELEMENTS:

Creative cycle: Wood feeds fire, fire gives life to the earth and produces metal, metal like all the minerals that the earth contains give life to water, which in turn nourishes the wood.

Production cycle: Water generates wood but wood runs out of water; wood generates fire but fire exhausts wood; the fire generates the earth but the earth exhausts the fire; the earth generates metal but metal exhausts the earth; metal generates water but water depletes the metal.

Destructive cycle: Water destroys fire; fire destroys metal; metal destroys wood; wood destroys the earth; the earth destroys the water. The destructive cycle allows us to understand how much the hostility between two elements leads to destruction and bad Feng Shui.

Harmonic and disharmonic correspondences between the Elements

Elements / Harmonic / Neutral / Disharmonic

Wood / Fire and Water / Earth / Metal

Fire / Wood and Water / Metal / Water

Earth / Metal and Fire / Water / Wood

Metal / Water and Earth / Wood / Fire

Water / Wood and Metal / Fire / Earth

The Five Elements in Feng Shui:

Energy - Color - Form - Material - Images

Wood - blue green - rectangle - wood - woods

Fire - red - triangle - synthetics - fire

Earth - yellow brown - square - ceramic - cultivated fields

Metal - gray white - oval circle - metals - black white photo

Water - blue black - wavy - water - sea and fish

The strongest energy flows are from the South and from the East, so the entrance to a shop, warehouse or even apartment enjoys a good supply of vital energy when it is oriented towards these two directions. The Feng Shui discipline holds that positive energy comes from the South and negative energy from the North.

The Five Elements:

Metal:

Metal is associated with wealth and protection, which has always been a symbol of protection, in some cultures metal objects are used to ward off negative influences. In Feng shui, metal is also a symbol of organization.

- Its location is WEST - NORTH WEST

- Bagua number: 6/7

- Its color is white, gray, metallic, gold, silver

- Its energy is Yang

- Its season is autumn

- Its shape is the circle (anything that is round or semi-round)

- The movement of its energy is inward

- The trigram of the West is called Tui

- The Northwest trigram is called Kienn

At home the North West is the ideal area for the bedroom of grandparents and influential people, in the company it is ideal for the executive office. The metal zone is also suitable as a laboratory and workshop.

For Feng Shui the precious metals are: stainless steel; aluminum; brass; silver; iron.

The Metal Person is clear and lucid mentally, loves minimalism and is very organized, loves to have fun, is charming, elegant, communicative and optimistic. A little bit of the fire element helps soften the temperament of the metal person.

FENG SHUI: HOME DESIGN AND COLORS

Metal is associated with money and this is perhaps the most commonly adopted form in China to enhance the element in question, these coins are often found to have a square hole in the center to be tied together by a red ribbon. These small groups of coins are placed at home, among documents or in the wallet as a symbol of luck and wealth.

Materials: All metallic objects, crystal, coins, these materials serve to stimulate the energy of the West. Smooth surfaces, round shapes and all shades of color ranging from gray to gold are suitable for Metal people.

The Stones in Feng Shui associated with the Metal Element are: hyaline quartz; turquoise; jade; lapis lazuli; sodalite; moonstone; eye of the Tiger.

Metal in relation to the other elements: (transformation phases)

Cycle of creation: Metal feeds Water (steam) - Earth feeds Metal (minerals)

Destruction cycle: Metal destroys Wood (sawing) - Water corrodes Metal

Earth:

The Earth element is of vital importance for Feng Shui and more, it is from the earth that we draw the raw materials for daily life and for survival. Our houses are built from materials that come from it, wood, clay, bricks, stones, not to mention the food products that the earth offers us for our livelihood. The Earth element is considered the most stable of the five. Even if the earth is hot and in its center there is incandescent lava, for Feng Shui it is a dry and cold element.

 - Its location is the South-West; Northeast, Center

 - Bagua number : 2/5/8

 - Its main color is yellow, brown, beige

 - Its energy is yin, therefore feminine, receptive and passive

 - Represents strength, resourcefulness, abundance, stability, reliability

 - Season: It does not have a season assigned as its strength is vital throughout the year

FENG SHUI: HOME DESIGN AND COLORS

- Its shape is the square, or rather all flat surfaces

- The movement of its energy is towards the center

- The Southwest trigram is called Kunn

- The Northeast trigram is called Kenn

The Earth element in Feng Shui stabilizes the balance in environments where there is a lot of energy movement. At home, materials such as ceramics, terracotta and stones are suitable for powering the Earth's energy. Placing plants near the front door is very conducive to the Chi of the house, then if the pots were made of terracotta, we will optimize all feng shui practices. The characteristic traits of the Earth Person are stability, practicality, reliability, industriousness, fertility, empathy, honesty, prudence. The emotions and qualities of an Earth personality are melancholy, worry, reflection and instinctive awareness. When the earth person is in a period of instability, he tends to accumulate things to restore balance, but unknowingly feeding a state of confusion and disorder. The Earth person, being altruistic, runs the risk of being exploited. The activities best suited to the Earth person include construction, real estate, food industry, services, marketing, stock exchange, banking and charity. The Land area of a site is suitable for closets, pantries, walk-in closets and greenhouses.

Materials: low furniture, long tables and comfortable sofas with large cushions, and all materials in terracotta, ceramic, clay, and brick. Keep these areas very tidy, remove objects belonging to the past.

The Stones in Feng Shui associated with the Earth Element: amethyst; carnelian; hyaline quartz; selenite; green aventurine.

Earth in relation to the other elements: (transformation phases)

Cycle of creation: Fire feeds the Earth (ash) - Earth creates Metal

Destruction cycle: Wood destroys the Earth (absorbs) - Metal reduces the Earth

FENG SHUI: HOME DESIGN AND COLORS

Fire:

The fire element is a symbol of energy and passion, it is an element of extreme importance.

- Its direction is the South

- Bagua number: 9

- The season is summer

- It has yang energy that tends upward

- The shape it is associated with is triangular

- Its color is red

- The Southern trigram is called Li and the I King

- According to the eight purposes of life, the southern area refers to fame and reputation

- The sacred animal of the South is the Red Phoenix, a mythical bird that stands in front of the house and is always on the lookout to scan the horizon, waiting for good news

Of the five elements in Feng Shui, fire is the one with the most Yang energy of all. It is necessary to pay some attention to its presence in a living or working structure, if there is too much presence of this energy you could feel a sense of impatience and impulsiveness. This is the reason why all the characteristics of this energy, especially in the bedroom, must be inserted very sparingly as the room is intended for rest. Despite its power, one should not be afraid to insert the fire element. If there is not enough of it in the environment or if there is too little of it, there could be states of laziness or lack of motivation. If the dominant element of your home were fire, a situation of energy imbalance should be countered by inserting the other four Feng Shui elements: water, wood, earth and metal. The importance of color in Feng Shui is fundamental to quickly rebalance the energy in the environments and also on the person. If you feel sad or physically debilitated to recharge immediately, dressing in red can be an excellent remedy. The Fire Person has the character qualities of charm and enthusiasm. They are natural leaders and have the innate ability to attract other people's attention. The negative aspects of such personalities can be restlessness and impulsiveness, if the Fire person wants to control his temperament, he can introduce some blue objects in the southern area of the house. The color of the water in this case would have the purpose of sedating his soul. Fire element is connected to the kitchen and heating systems

Materials: plastic, animal materials, red colored objects.

The Stones in Feng Shui associated with the Fire Element: carnelian; citrine quartz; purpurite: ruby: bull's eye; red jasper.

Fire in relation to the other elements: (transformation phases)

Cycle of creation: Fire nourishes the Earth (ash) - It is nourished by Wood (fuel)

Cycle of Destruction: Fire Melts Metal - Fire is extinguished by Water

Wood:

The Wood Element represents growth, development and planning. The importance of this element for Feng Shui is given by the fact that its energy symbolically encloses that of the whole universe, it is associated with vitality and positive energy.

- It has Yang energy

- Bagua number: 3/4

- The cardinal point associated with wood is EAST - SOUTH EAST

- The movement of its energy tends upwards and outwards

- The shape is cylindrical

- The season it is associated with is spring

FENG SHUI: HOME DESIGN AND COLORS

- Its color is green and brown

- The trigram of the East is called Cenn

- The Southeast trigram is called Sunn

If we wanted to visualize the energy of wood, we could think of spring which heralds a new cycle of life. It is the earth that awakens. It is always recommended to have plants positioned near the main door of the house, whoever enters will feel welcome and whoever leaves will keep a good memory of the house and of those who live there, even the smell that plants and flowers emit contribute to the well-being of those who live in that environment favoring harmony and balance. The Wood Person has many characteristics, is open, optimistic, exuberant, full of new ideas, is kind, generous, expansive, gives a lot of importance to ethical and moral values, has a lot of self-confidence, knows how to recognize the intrinsic value of things and for this reason he is predisposed to do things big. They are personalities suitable for carrying out scientific studies, they work well in groups and are able to find solutions to problems. They just don't finish what they start, jumping from one project to another without completing it. Wooden objects, rectangular and vertical shapes adapt to the furniture of a Wood person. The area to the east of the house is suitable for children and for studying. In the offices, the East is the best area for research, innovation and programming. The South East area is suitable for carrying out tasks related to money and diplomacy as it is associated with wealth and prosperity. The wood element is suitable for the dining room and the children's bedroom

Materials: all wooden objects, bamboo, wooden furniture, tall plants, and any painting that symbolizes upward movement.

The Stones in Feng Shui associated with the Wood Element: amethyst; shungite; turquoise; green tourmaline; carnelian; turquoise; agate.

Wood in relation to the other elements: (transformation phase)

Cycle of creation: Wood feeds Fire - Wood is nourished by Water

Destruction cycle: Wood destroys the Earth (roots) - Wood is depleted by Metal

FENG SHUI: HOME DESIGN AND COLORS

Water:

The Water element. As you know, Feng Shui means "Wind and Water" which were originally considered the generating energies of the whole universe, and from here it can be deduced that this is a very significant element also for our life. In ancient times, cities were built along the edges of rivers to facilitate the transport of goods and the resulting trade was a source of wealth for entire populations. Even today, in companies, shops and businesses in general, the northern area is associated with the element of water and is considered a good omen for business. The direction of the North symbolizes career, money and economic well-being.

- Water is the Yin element

- Bagua number: 1

- It is associated with the north cardinal point

- To the color black, blue, turquoise, light blue, silver and gold

- The Northern trigram is called Kan

- Its energy is associated with the concentric shape

- Its shape is irregular

- the season it is associated with is Winter

- The colors are Black and Blue

- For Feng Shui this element is closely linked to the wisdom of the soul

- The northern area of the house is suitable for the bedroom, meditation and bathroom

- The animal referred to in the direction of the North is the Black Turtle

We are all largely made up of water, us humans, and the planet earth we inhabit. It is also indispensable for reproduction, in fact without it there would be no fertilization. To work at its best, water energy needs a movement that tends downwards in nature, and a flow that, in order to be optimized, must follow a sinuous and not direct trend. In reading the areas of a house for Feng Shui, you will notice an association between bathrooms and wealth precisely because of their correspondence to the water element. The water in Feng Shui is fed with fountains or aquariums, the important thing is to always keep the water fresh and clear.

The Water Person is associated with a calm and reflective character, giving the person a tendency to seek the deep meaning of things and quickly leave out everything that does not interest them.

Properly applied water energy for Feng Shui can strengthen existing relationships, help create new relationships, and aid a home's prosperity. A painting depicting scenes with water can, like an aquarium, be a good omen for economic activity. The Water Element is suitable for the bathroom, the laundry room, the study room.

Materials: mirrors, plastic, glass, paintings depicting scenes with water, aquariums, fountains.

The Stones in Feng Shui associated with the Water Element: azure; black tourmaline; blue jade; Hawk eye; carnelian; hyaline quartz; hematite.

Water in relation to the other elements: (transformation phase)

Cycle of creation: Metal feeds Water (minerals) - Water feeds Wood (plants)

Destruction cycle: Water destroys Fire (extinguishes) - Earth runs out of Water

Whenever you feel energetically drained, get in touch with your Element

If you are Earth you will need to have a contact with nature; if you are Water, visit the sea, a lake or a river; if you are Metal, carry an object of gold or silver with you; if you are Wood visit a museum or a place of culture, if you are Fire burn some incense or light a bonfire.

FENG SHUI: HOME DESIGN AND COLORS

CONCLUSION

FENG SHUI GUIDELINES FOR HOME FURNISHING

Furnishing your home without the help of a professional can be complicated: the choice of style, arrangement of furnishings and accessories is a complex matter in front of which you can find yourself confused: it happened to me too, at the beginning, with the furniture of my new home. But there is a philosophy coming from the Far East that can guide us in these operations: feng shui. This practice, founded in China, also fascinates Westerners a lot, because it is associated with a style of furnishing similar to minimalism. Without pretending to dissect it in its totality and complexity, here are some tips, which in turn have been given to me, to make the furnishings of the house balanced and harmonious.

This discipline, started over 5000 years ago, consists of a set of practices for reading spaces, be they landscapes or rooms in a house. Following the principles of beauty, harmony and balance, feng shui indicates how to organize the environment and objects inside them, in order to eliminate negative flows that can affect people's lives.

In particular, according to feng shui, the house is the "container of man", the building with which he has the closest bond and which must therefore adapt to his character and lifestyle. Fascinating, right? Now let's arm ourselves with a compass and see some rules for feng shui decor.

The feng shui entrance

According to feng shui, the front door of the house corresponds to the man's mouth: through the entrance one is introduced into the flow of positive energy of the house. This is why it is important that the door opens inwards and that no stairs, bathrooms or mirrors are placed in front of it. Rather than with a mirror, feng shui recommends decorating the entrance with paintings, which must represent natural elements, such as landscapes, flowers or animals. To avoid religious images and images that represent weapons, because they recall

FENG SHUI: HOME DESIGN AND COLORS

loneliness and violence. As for the colors of the entrance, feng shui indicates white, blue, green and pink as appropriate.

The feng shui kitchen

The kitchen is a vital place, where basic daily activities such as preparing meals and eating take place. To accommodate the energy present in this room, the most suitable color is yellow. Feng shui poses very stringent rules regarding the placement of the kitchen: it must not be near the entrance of the house and the door to access it must not be opposite the stove. It is also essential that the kitchen is tidy: put away unnecessary objects and decorations that are better reserved for other rooms in the house.

The feng shui living room

The living room is the room in the house where guests are welcomed and time is spent in company: the arrangement of the furniture and the colors must therefore favor conversations and a family atmosphere. The sofa must be positioned close to the wall and must not face openings such as doors and windows, from which too powerful flows of energy could enter. The most suitable colors for a feng shui living room are red and orange.

Furthermore, with the right accessories, the living area of the house can be transformed into a do-it-yourself relaxation room: just add meditation or yoga cushions and spread some essences in the room to meditate, with incense, diffusers and scented candles.

Even in the living room the element of water must not be missing: an excellent idea is therefore to introduce an aquarium. In addition to harmonizing the environment, according to feng shui, the aquarium is one of the objects that bring wealth! The rules? Arrange it on the east side of the house (the direction associated with money) and populate it with goldfish which, according to Chinese beliefs, are able to attract money.

The feng shui bedroom

Have you ever thought about it? The bedroom is the room in the house where we spend the most time: usually from 6 to 8 consecutive hours. It goes without saying, therefore, that feng shui pays a lot of attention to the decor of this environment.

First of all, feng shui takes into account the position of the bed, which must be placed on the right side of the room, opposite the entrance. The ideal bed orientation is with the headboard facing south and the footboard should never be facing a door or mirror.

A curiosity that not many know: according to feng shui, the edges of the furniture generate negative energy, so it is important that they are never turned towards the bed. Finally, for the bedroom, feng shui recommends soft colors such as blue and white.

The feng shui bathroom

The bathroom is the place where you take care of yourself, so it must be bright and harmonious. The feng shui tradition is based on the balance between the elements of nature: water, earth, fire, metal and wood. In the bathroom, the main element is water, which must be balanced with the use of wooden furniture and decorative plants: in this way you will obtain an elegant and refined Zen-style bathroom. A perfect accessory for a feng shui bathroom is... music! Bring a small stereo or a speaker to the bathroom, immerse yourself in the tub and play a compilation of oriental music at low volume: relaxation is guaranteed! The perfect color for a feng shui bathroom is green.

Other feng shui spaces

Feng shui office

There are also other environments to consider. The office, for example: whether it's a room in your home or in another building, you can furnish it to make it a harmonious place that promotes concentration and creativity. The feng shui rules to keep in mind in the office are few and easy to follow: work facing natural light sources such as windows and doors, keep your desk tidy and place any electrical appliance at least 50 cm away from you.

FENG SHUI: HOME DESIGN AND COLORS

Moving outside the house, finally, we find the garden. To respect feng shui, all the elements of nature must be present: earth, rock, wood and water. If you have the opportunity, you can build a small fountain or an artificial pond. As for the vegetation, feng shui prefers spontaneous ones; if you want to plant trees or flowers, that's fine, as long as they are in season or evergreen, a symbol of longevity. To decorate the garden, we turn to nature: stones from seas or rivers should be used, preferably in an odd number, to be arranged in an orderly manner in various points of the garden. These in fact, represent real good luck objects for feng shui.

In short, there are many rules to keep in mind to get the ideal feng shui house, but you need only adopt a few to bring a touch of the Orient to your home, wherever it is.

Printed in Great Britain
by Amazon